FERRARI

the battle for revival

Other books by the same author

WILLIAMS
Triumph out of Tragedy

DAMON HILL
From Zero to Hero

THE QUEST FOR SPEED
Modern Racing Car Design and Technology

DRIVING FORCES
Fifty Men Who Have Shaped Motor Racing

WILLIAMS
The Business of Grand Prix Racing

FIFTY FAMOUS MOTOR RACES

DEREK BELL
My Racing Life

FERRARI
The Grand Prix Cars

BRABHAM
The Grand Prix Cars

MARCH
The Grand Prix and Indy Cars

JACKIE STEWART'S PRINCIPLES
OF PERFORMANCE DRIVING

As part of our ongoing market research, we are always pleased to receive comments about our books, suggestions for new titles, or requests for catalogues. Please write to: The Editorial Director, Patrick Stephens Limited, Sparkford, Nr Yeovil, Somerset BA22 7JJ.

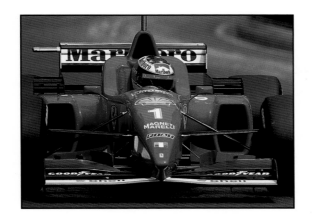

FERRARI

the battle for revival

BY ALAN HENRY
Foreword by Niki Lauda

Patrick Stephens Limited

First published in 1996

British Library Cataloguing-in-Publication Data:
A catalogue record for this book is available from the British Library

ISBN: 1 85260 552 9

Library of Congress catalog card no. 96-75816

Patrick Stephens Limited is an imprint of Haynes Publishing, Sparkford, Nr Yeovil, Somerset BA22 7JJ.

Designed and typeset by Camway Autographics, Sparkford, Somerset BA22 7JJ.
Printed in Hong Kong.

Contents

Acknowledgements

I would like to thank all those members of the Ferrari 'family' who have found time to talk to me, on or off the record, at various Grands Prix over the years during which the core of this story was developing. Most notably they include Luca di Montezemolo, Jean Todt, Gerhard Berger, Jean Alesi, Niki Lauda and Michael Schumacher.

I must also single out John Barnard for special thanks. He generously hosted a visit to Ferrari Design & Development which enabled me to gain a much deeper understanding of the challenges facing Maranello's UK-based F1 design satellite, in addition to the overall intricacies of contemporary Grand Prix car design.

Thanks also to Michael Harvey, Editor of *Autocar*, and Peter Foubister, publisher of *Autosport*, for permission to quote from those two periodicals. Also to Steven Tee and Kathy Agar of LAT Photographic, ICN UK Bureau, Allsport, Darren Heath, and Tim Watson of Ferrari UK for their help in sourcing and organising the photographic content contained within these covers.

Foreword by Niki Lauda

World Champion 1975, 1977 and 1984

I first became associated with Ferrari when Luca di Montezemolo approached me on behalf of the company in the summer of 1973, offering a contract to drive in their Formula 1 team in the following season's World Championship programme. As a hungry young driver out to make his name, I naturally jumped at the chance and was dazzled by the resources the team apparently had at its disposal.

With the team under Luca's guidance, I was fortunate to play a part in one of Ferrari's most successful spells of Grand Prix achievement. Now, some 20 years later, circumstances have led me back into an association with the team on an advisory basis.

Ferrari is and will always be one of the most fascinating, charismatic, unpredictable and colourful teams on the Grand Prix trail. In this book Alan Henry has attempted to explain how the foundations were put into place for what is intended to be a period of sustained success for the Prancing Horse. Time alone will tell how successful all our efforts have been.

March, 1996

Straight from the grid

Crowds burst over the spectator fences and poured on to the circuit as the cars began their slowing down laps at the end of the 1996 San Marino Grand Prix. On the one hand it was good, old-fashioned pro-Ferrari hysteria, on the other, a dangerous lack of collective discipline which would result in the Imola circuit organisers being called to account in front of the sport's governing body.

Yet this upwelling of spontaneous enthusiasm could be taken as a signal to motor racing enthusiasts all over the world – Ferrari had returned as a potential F1 winning force.

This much-vaunted Grand Prix revival was the result of a massive investment in engineering and design input, organisational structure and, perhaps most important of all, a world-class number one driver in the person of Michael Schumacher.

For the second successive weekend, the double World Champion had finished second to a Williams-Renault. At Nurburgring the previous Sunday he had played a very close second fiddle to Jacques Villeneuve. Now, at Imola's Autodromo Enzo e Dino Ferrari, it had been Damon Hill who was first past the chequered flag. Yet somehow that detail hardly mattered to the exultant *tifosi*.

Thanks to Schumacher's brilliance at the wheel of the latest John Barnard-designed F310, Maranello was at last poised to go the final mile which, for so many years, had separated them as 'best of the rest' from that select band of race winners. True, the Prancing Horse had enjoyed a few fleeting moments in the sun. Gerhard Berger had triumphed at Hockenheim in 1994, Jean Alesi in Montreal the following year. But this time you could sense that there was a consistency underpinning the prospect of greater things to come. Ferrari were now serious contenders for the World Championship.

When Michael Schumacher had decided to leave Benetton at the end of 1995 after winning back-to-back World Championships, he did so because he wanted a fresh challenge. Coincidentally, Ferrari were looking for an absolute top driver. A two-year contract was forged, guaranteeing Schumacher slightly more than $40 million dollars for the 32 races which would make up the 1996 and 1997 Grand Prix seasons.

One electrifying element of Ferrari's revival is that the famous Italian team has given the 26-year old German a launching pad from which he could very well become the highest-earning sportsman in the world. According to informed sources, a couple of sweeps of the contractual pen should ensure that he surges from ninth place to pole position in the dollar-earning stakes.

With a $20 million annual retainer from Ferrari topped up by $5 million from his personal sponsors plus a $20 million endorsement deal from Nike, he could take home around $45 million by the end of the 1996 season. Thus he may leap ahead of basketball legend Michael Jordan ($43.9 million), boxer Mike Tyson ($40 million), Dallas Cowboys footballer Delon Sanders ($22.5 million), Riddick Bowe ($22.2 million), basketballer Shaquille O'Neal ($21.9 million), George Foreman ($18 million), tennis star Andre Agassi ($16 million) and golfer Jack Niklaus ($15.1 million). Nice work if you can get it.

Yet the reason that Ferrari has been prepared to commit to such a massive investment is that Michael Schumacher is truly The Man Who Makes the Difference. The consensus within the F1 community is that Schumacher is worth the best part of one second a lap over any contemporary rival driving a similar car. That is night and day in terms of F1 competitiveness.

In essence, by signing Schumacher, Ferrari has eliminated one crucial variable from the complex equation involved in running a Grand Prix team. They can now assume that if their car is not quick enough, then the blame certainly cannot be laid at the door of their number one driver. Schumacher is not only the quickest driver in the business, he is also consistent, intelligent and analytical. In short, he is the best of the bunch.

The Ferrari team has laboured long and hard to assemble a team capable of challenging for the World Championship. This volume recounts the full details involved in struggling along what has been a long road of painful, emotional and protracted development.

Maranello's slog back into the limelight has been continuing since 1990 when Alain Prost won five races and came within hailing distance of the World Championship before his ambitions were abruptly terminated at Suzuka when Ayrton Senna, in a McLaren, rammed him off the track. It was an episode which left an indelible mark both on the sport as a whole and on Senna's otherwise outstanding record of achievement. In many ways it was also a defining moment, the occasion when many people concluded that sportsmanship in F1 went out of the window for good and all. From now on, it became business – first, second, and last.

Of course, those with a taste for motor racing history are sufficiently shrewd to appreciate that, for the late Enzo Ferrari, motor racing was not simply passion and commitment alone.

The Commendatore, who died in 1988, ruled his empire with a well-honed, commercially opportunistic zeal. He manipulated the media, intimidated his employees and left many of his drivers in a state of fear and trembling.

While much has changed within the Ferrari F1 team since the passing of the man whose name it still carries, a great deal certainly has not. Yet it is this rare blend of enthusiasm, intrigue, romance, nostalgia, commitment and determination which somehow continues to ensure that Ferrari's Grand Prix cars are surrounded by an aura of almost magical – some would say misplaced – fascination.

This book recounts the latest chapter in the ongoing drama.

Overleaf: Glorious moment – Michael Schumacher's Ferrari F310 (1) accelerates away from pole position at the start of the 1996 San Marino GP ahead of the Williams-Renaults of Damon Hill (left) and Jacques Villeneuve. It was the team's first pole at the Autodromo Enzo e Dino Ferrari for 13 years (ICN UK Bureau).

Chapter One

A championship lost

The story of Ferrari's 1990 World Championship near-miss has its roots in the decision – taken in the summer of 1986 – fundamentally to re-structure the team. At about that time John Barnard, then Chief Designer at McLaren, was seeking to leave the team, his working relationship with co-director Ron Dennis having deteriorated to the point where it was no longer tenable.

John's CV at the sharp edge of international motor racing design technology was wide-ranging and well-established. After an early career with Lola and McLaren, he made his name during the mid-1970s engineering the ambitious Vel's Parnelli IndyCars in the USA. Among the pioneering technical developments he had been closely involved with were the first turbo-charged version of the Cosworth V8 engine and a transverse gearbox development for the California-based team.

Later he designed the Chaparral 2K which won the 1979 Indy 500, before returning to England and joining forces with Ron Dennis to take over the operation of the fading McLaren F1 team at the behest of its prime sponsor, Philip Morris, the cigarette conglomerate. McLaren hadn't won a race in three years when Dennis and Barnard effectively took control mid-way through 1980. A year later the newly titled McLaren International organisation put the marque back on the winning map when John Watson triumphed in the British Grand Prix at Silverstone.

Barnard had consolidated his reputation as an audacious and imaginative engineer by adopting carbon-fibre composite chassis construction for the new McLaren MP4 chassis, but this was just a starting point. In the years that followed, he refined and developed this concept as well as outlining the specification of the Porsche-built TAG turbo 1.5-litre V6 engine which McLaren commissioned the German company to produce to John's rigid design guidelines. The McLaren-TAGs then sprinted to a hat-trick of World Championships from 1984 to 1986, but Barnard was not there when Alain Prost clinched the third of those titles with victory in the Australian GP at Adelaide.

The problems which eventually led to the breakdown of the Dennis/Barnard alliance reflected the fact that the two men were alike in many ways. Both were no-compromise perfectionists in their personal spheres of operation – Dennis on the commercial and administrative side, Barnard when it came to design and engineering.

Yet despite their similarities the two men frequently disagreed. The noise of their vociferous exchanges often sent colleagues running for cover and soon passed into motor racing folklore. Barnard had by now sold his shareholding in the company to Mansour Ojjeh, scion of the Franco-Lebanese family which now controlled McLaren through the TAG Group, and decided he had no choice but to leave.

Nigel Mansell's Ferrari 640 during the opening stages of the 1989 Brazilian GP. After a troubled time during practice and qualifying, Mansell won first time out in the distinctive new John Barnard-designed contender (LAT).

Barnard was not lacking when it came to offers of alternative employment. He had been discussing the prospect of an ambitious F1 programme with BMW, but confesses that he was intrigued when he received a mystery approach from an intermediary for what was described as a 'prominent F1 team'.

The deal almost fell at the first hurdle. John was asked if he would relocate to Europe. His answer was firmly in the negative. He had a wife and young family, all of whom were settled into home and education in Surrey. The idea of leaving England simply didn't appeal.

It appears that the intermediary was not put off. Back came a formal proposition, but again Barnard stalled. By this stage he was fairly certain in his own mind that Ferrari was behind the offer, but it also crossed his mind that it could be Peugeot or Renault, both of whom had been toying with the idea of initiating new F1 programmes. Finally, Ferrari's man identified himself and a revised deal was put on the table. Would John be interested if he could be based in the UK? On that basis, he met team director Marco Piccinini to discuss the matter in more detail.

Out of all the subsequent negotiations was born Ferrari's first F1 design satellite, GTO, based at a new business park in Shalford, near Guildford. GTO stood for Guildford Technical Office – although many observers regarded it as an excruciatingly corny acronym bearing in mind that those initials, GTO, had been the designation of one of the company's most famous sports racing cars in the 1960s. As Chief Designer Barnard had the task of mapping out Ferrari's long-term F1 future, with particular emphasis on the 3.5-litre naturally-aspirated engine regulations which would supplant the 1.5-litre turbos at the start of 1989.

The next couple of years would prove difficult in the extreme for Barnard. As Ferrari's turbo effort gradually played itself out, he had to concentrate not only on a radical new design concept, but also spent much time fending off the waspish political jealousy surfacing from rivals within the ranks at Maranello.

The first such disruption occurred in the summer of 1987 after team driver Michele Alboreto went public with criticism of Barnard's modus operandi. The Italian described Barnard as being 'like a brain surgeon attempting a complicated operation over the telephone'. The Italian media picked up on this, fuelling the feverish row to the point where the senior management at Fiat – which owns Ferrari – were so intimidated that John had to take time off from design work on the new 3.5-litre challenger and travel to Hockenheim for what amounted to an impromptu trial by press. There were people in F1 who questioned this response, feeling that it did not add up to the sort of confident, cohesive operation expected of a front-line team with championship aspirations. All in all, it was a counter-productive exercise.

For 1988 the FIA, the sport's governing body, intended a year of transition with new 3.5-litre cars permitted to compete for the first time and the 1.5-litre turbos also allowed, but with their power output hopefully capped by a new 2.5-bar boost limitation allied to a 150-litre fuel capacity maximum. With Barnard's new 639 development running behind schedule, Maranello decided to stay with the turbos for this final year, but high hopes were comprehensively dashed when the new McLaren-Hondas emerged to win 15 out of the season's 16 races. Ferrari at least had the consolation of a 1-2 in the Italian Grand Prix at Monza, but that was as far as it went.

Meanwhile, Barnard's new machine was gradually taking shape behind the scenes, but this did not appear for its first tests until July 1988. Visually distinguished by its high

Mansell can't believe his good fortune as he takes his place on the rostrum at Rio. Yet this magical start was not to set the overall tone for his Ferrari career (LAT).

side pods which extended almost to the rear of the front wheels, the type 639 test car was propelled by a brand-new 65-degree V12 engine with a bore and stroke of 84.4mm x 52.6mm for a capacity of 3497.6cc.

With a compression ratio of 11.5:1 it was claimed that the new engine would develop 600bhp at 12,500rpm by the time its serious development testing began later in the year. But more interesting by far was the new Ferrari's transmission. Barnard's new machine was equipped with a radical electronically activated change mechanism for its seven-speed gearbox.

His concept incorporated a pair of levers behind the steering wheel which would allow the drivers to change gear using only finger-tip pressure, relaying an electronic message via a control box to an otherwise conventional, but hydraulically operated, gearbox.

This was the car which would be developed into the definitive Ferrari 640 and would continue to distinguish itself by being a first-time winner on its race debut the following year. However, in the process of finalising the type 640's specification, Barnard experienced a high-level confrontation with Maranello's senior management who got a last-minute attack of the jitters over the prospect of his semi-automatic gearchange. He should, they suggested, develop a manual gearbox version.

Insiders at Fiat – which owned Ferrari – confirmed that this dispute very nearly became a resignation issue. Barnard made it clear that unless he had unequivocal support for his new car, there was little point in continuing to work for Maranello. It was easy to see why Barnard was so trenchant in his defence of the new system. Its biggest advantage was that the clutch was not disengaged for a milli-second longer than necessary, facilitating gearchanges far faster than could be achieved by a driver using a conventional linkage. In purely practical terms, even if each such individual change was

Gerhard Berger negotiates the tight chicane during the 1989 Belgian GP meeting. The Austrian had a troubled season with the type 640, marred by a fiery accident at Imola and brightened by only a single win at Estoril (Allsport).

John Barnard (right) and Alain Prost (left) with McLaren engineer Tim Wright. John and Alain had enjoyed a tremendous working relationship at McLaren between 1984 and 1986, but Alain only signed for Ferrari in 1990 a couple of months after John's departure (LAT).

one-tenth of a second faster, the time saved over a race distance could, in theory, prove decisive – well in excess of 10 seconds.

In addition, there was a safety element to consider as the driver never had to take his hands off the steering wheel, a saving in complexity with the elimination of the gear linkage and aerodynamic benefits from the resultant narrower cockpit. Furthermore, the car's fundamental performance bottom line was underpinned by excellent aerodynamics which, in turn, contributed to an impressive turn of straight-line speed.

The new Ferrari was powered by a brand-new 3.5-litre V12, the design parameters of which Barnard had outlined with the same meticulous care as had been lavished on the Porsche-made TAG turbo concept. 'I decided on a 12-cylinder engine on the basis that we needed to go for the ultimate power option,' he explained. 'In effect I was telling them to give me the power and I would package the unit in the best possible way. We originally thought of a 60-degree layout, but opened it out by another five degrees in order to give space for more ancillaries within the vee, and I also requested that all the pumps should be neatly positioned at the front, just like the Porsche V6.'

For Ferrari, the 1989 and 1990 seasons would also be suffused with optimism on the driver front with Nigel Mansell and Alain Prost entering the fold at the start of those two respective years. Both men were intent on revitalising already distinguished F1 careers which had either stalled or encountered temporary setbacks for one reason or another.

Mansell's decision to join Ferrari at the start of 1989 was motivated by an urge to establish himself once and for all in the F1 front-line and take what promised to be a realistic tilt at the World Championship. It was also a decision prompted by a desire to move from Williams after a dismally disappointing 1988 season wrestling with Judd V8 engines after Honda had pulled the plug on its works engine deal at the end of the previous season.

Now approaching his 35th birthday, Mansell was anxious for sustained success. The moustachioed Englishman – one of the old-style hard-chargers, with a fan club to match – was always a highly emotional sportsman. Yet the knee-jerk philosophy which apparently guided many of his career decisions could not totally conceal the fact that he was a shrewd businessman who was becoming increasingly accomplished at turning negotiating positions to his own commercial advantage.

Moreover, there was a question of personal esteem to be considered. Mansell was a proud man who, some felt rightly, believed his solid record of achievement in the Williams-Honda squad from 1985–87 entitled him to rather more reverential regard than the British team's management was willing to give. Frank Williams and his Technical Director Patrick Head were both down-to-earth motor racing pragmatists who had fought a successful 10-year battle to establish their team at the very pinnacle of F1 achievement. To describe them as unsentimental would be unnecessarily pejorative, yet although they admired Mansell enormously for his brilliance at the wheel, they were not always temperamentally in tune when Nigel was out of the cockpit.

Tantalised by the prospect of the new John Barnard-designed Ferrari 640, Mansell accepted a handsome financial package from Ferrari – believed to be in the region of $4 million – and went forward to embrace the effusive adulation which was virtually guaranteed by his switch to Maranello. His team-mate there was Gerhard Berger, in his third season with the team.

The following year, Prost would have subtly different considerations in mind when he joined Ferrari. Having won consecutive World Championships in 1985 and 1986, he had come to be regarded as an absolutely central element within the McLaren team. In many ways, McLaren was his family; he'd made his Grand Prix debut there in 1980 and, despite leaving for a three-year sojourn with Renault, returned at the start of 1984.

But things had begun to change for Prost at the start of 1988 when McLaren became beneficiaries of the Williams team's misfortune and picked up not only the Honda engine deal but also the services of the highly motivated Ayrton Senna. Within 18 months, the Brazilian had effectively undermined Prost's confidence to the point that Alain, mid-way through 1989, announced that he would be leaving McLaren at the end of the season. Initially it seemed as though he might be toying with retirement, but events unfolded to ensure that he gained a high-profile seat at Ferrari alongside Mansell from the start of 1990.

However, Prost's breach with McLaren was some months away when Mansell opened the 1989 season with a slightly fortuitous victory in the Brazilian GP at Rio. The Ferrari 640 had been bugged with technical problems through both qualifying sessions to the point that Mansell booked himself and his wife Rosanne on the British Airways flight back to Europe leaving at 4.30pm on the afternoon of the race.

The car would only last a handful of laps, he reasoned, giving him just enough time to take a helicopter to the airport with sufficient to spare. As things transpired, the Ferrari 640 never missed a beat in the race and he stormed home a convincing winner. At a stroke, Nigel had established himself as an Italian national hero, the latest in a long line of British drivers to taste success at the wheel of one of Maranello's finest.

Mansell's victory in Brazil also served to staunch some of the intra-team criticism which had been directed at John Barnard's imaginative approach to the type 640's overall engineering – particularly its semi-automatic gearbox system.

'Although the basic gearbox functions satisfactorily, there are still problems

Can Schuey follow Fangio's lead?

It was one of those familiar, brilliantly sunny afternoons at Monza. The date, 9 September 1979; the occasion, the Italian Grand Prix. In the closing stages of the race the crowd held its breath, watching in a mood of awe tinged with disbelief. For the first time in four long years, a Ferrari driver was going to win the World Championship.

At the chequered flag, Jody Scheckter would cross the finishing line 1.2sec ahead of his team-mate Gilles Villeneuve. At the age of 29, the South African driver had at last realised the dream which had been driving his raw ambition ever since he'd arrived in Britain to race a Formula Ford car just over eight years earlier. Those who watched Scheckter climb the ladder to F1 stardom were never in any doubt that the tousle-haired youngster from East London had what it took to scale the summits of Grand Prix achievement. Now he had completed the job and was on top of the world.

If, amid the chaotic, milling throng in the paddock celebrating Scheckter's victory, anybody had suggested that he would be the last World Champion to gain his crown at the wheel of a Ferrari for almost two decades, he would have been dismissed as a pessimistic eccentric. Or perhaps even lynched, such was the mood of emotional overload. Yet the ebb and flow of Grand Prix fortune would prove cruelly, bitterly, disappointing to the famous Maranello brigade in the years that followed.

In 1996 the arrival of double World Champion Michael Schumacher to head the driver line-up was hailed by the Ferrari faithful as salvation at last. Apart from the German's own glittering record of achievement with Benetton – talent that would surely now empower the Prancing Horse – there was a comforting precedent from which to draw hope.

The previous occasion when a reigning World Champion was recruited from another team to drive for the Prancing Horse was in 1956. Juan Manuel Fangio joined from Mercedes-Benz and that season duly won his third title. In a Ferrari.

Forty years later, Maranello would find itself hoping against hope that Michael Schumacher would manage to achieve the same distinction.

involving broken wires to the electro-valves within the control system that we must rectify quickly,' he admitted. Nevertheless, this initial taste of victory champagne in no way altered Barnard's pragmatic approach to the business of F1 racing with Ferrari. For the second race at Imola, he braced himself for the hysteria and uncompromising mood of expectancy which always erupts when Ferrari turns out to do battle on its home patch.

As expected, McLaren set the pace with Senna and Prost buttoning up the front row of the grid for the start of what promised to be a highly controversial confrontation between the two Honda-propelled drivers. As Prost and Senna scrapped for the lead, Mansell settled down to run third from the start ahead of Riccardo Patrese's Williams and Berger in the other Ferrari.

At the start of lap four, powering into the long Tamburello left-hander beyond the pits, Gerhard suddenly felt something give way at the front of his 640. In a split-second the car became uncontrollable and, instead of sweeping through the turn on the racing line, speared straight on towards the wall. Mercifully, the car impacted against the concrete wall with a glancing blow, but it was enough to send Berger ricocheting down the wall for more than 100 metres.

The 640 shed bodywork, wings and wheels before coming to rest, but the initial impact had forced the right-hand side radiator back into the front of the fuel cell running along the right-hand side of the cockpit. The carbon-fibre composite chassis deformed progressively to absorb the enormous impact, and was completely destroyed. The tank immediately began leaking its 200-litre fuel load and the car erupted into a fireball. The horror of those flames, from which surely no driver could escape alive, will be an enduring image for 1989. And a tribute to circuit management.

Gerhard owed his survival to the superb Imola safety services. Within 15 seconds of the car coming to rest, the crew of an Alfa Romeo 164 fire tender were on the scene and it took them only another eight seconds to quell the conflagration. The Austrian driver was taken to the circuit medical centre for body scans and X-rays before being transferred to Bologna's Maggiore hospital suffering from a broken rib, a lineal fracture of the left shoulder blade, chemical burns to his torso and second-degree burns to his hands.

Quite naturally, the race was red-flagged to a halt. When it was later restarted, Mansell alone represented Maranello. He lasted just 23 of the race's 58 laps, retiring from third place behind the McLarens with a gearbox failure. That was an irrelevant footnote to the weekend's activities, however. The feeling in the Ferrari camp was one of overwhelming relief that Gerhard had escaped so lightly.

Even so, Mansell was understandably seeking reassurance that his own car would not suffer a similarly catastrophic failure at the restart. The atmosphere in the back of the Ferrari transporter was electric as Barnard sought to calm Nigel's fears, yet at the same time knowing he was not in a position to offer an absolute, cast-iron assurance.

Racing cars are complex creatures, often unpredictable in the way they react to given situations. Nigel wanted to race but was well wound up about the whole affair. Eventually he made a balanced judgement and decided to go for it, his burning competitive spirit ruthlessly pushing any nagging doubts to the back of his mind.

Meanwhile Barnard's most urgent task was to assess how Berger's accident had been caused. He was deeply disturbed by the sequence of events which led Gerhard into such a highly vulnerable situation and eventually concluded that the left front aerofoil had sheared off the car, leaving him with a major aerodynamic imbalance at more than 180mph. This verdict tallied with evidence offered by Williams driver Thierry Boutsen who reported that he had seen some debris flying up from one of the cars running ahead of him as the pack accelerated towards Tamburello on the fateful lap.

Barnard concluded: 'Since the start of the 1988 season we had been running non-flexible front-wing end plates because there was some concern that the flexible ones might infringe the regulation which prohibited movable aerodynamic devices.

'In order to improve the wings' performance, we stiffened them up slightly, obviously reducing their deflection capability. I can't say how many laps that particular wing did over the Imola weekend, but clearly it became progressively over-strained and eventually broke off. That left Gerhard grappling with massive – and sudden – understeer.'

There were other thoughts which Barnard kept private. His years at McLaren with Lauda and Prost during the early 1980s had spoiled him to some degree. Whereas Niki and Alain were always scrupulous about keeping away from high kerbs – and, indeed, would mention specifically any such transgression on their next visit to the pit lane – Mansell and Berger were distinctly less inhibited. These two effervescent talents tended to regard kerbs as logical extensions of the race track, not always with predictable technical consequences.

Behind the scenes, tension was building between Barnard and Maranello's senior management. In June, during the week following the Canadian GP at Montreal, it was announced that the Englishman's volatile three-year stint as the team's Technical Director would terminate at the end of October 1989.

Prost celebrates his 40th Grand Prix victory in the spring of 1990. But there was no championship title awaiting him at Maranello (LAT).

PROST
40
1980-1990

Previous pages: Start of the 1990 Portuguese GP at Estoril, the race which caused a crucial breach between Nigel Mansell and his new team-mate Alain Prost. The two Ferraris had started from the front row of the grid, but at the green light Mansell swerved towards Prost and allowed the McLarens of Ayrton Senna and Gerhard Berger to get the jump on them both (LAT).

A formal communiqué from the team's headquarters announced a parting of the ways for the perfectionist engineer and the temperamental Italian car maker which already had a long tradition of falling out with its key employees. Barnard, it was announced, would be succeeded by Argentinian engineer Enrique Scalabroni, formerly a member of the Williams design team. It was planned that he should join the team at the start of September as Chief Engineer, his tenure overlapping with Barnard for just a month.

'I have no plans yet decided for the future,' said Barnard in response to the announcement. A recent meeting between him and Ferrari President Piero Fusaro had covered a number of possibilities for continuing the relationship, although it was clear that his refusal to be based in Italy had now emerged as the main problem.

However, Ferrari's somewhat clumsy attempts to sanction Barnard in this matter seemed to ignore the obvious fact that the team had been happy enough to accept his demand for a UK base originally. 'It was an absolutely central element of our arrangement from the outset,' said John. 'If they had insisted I went there from the start of our relationship, there would never have been any deal at all. They kept GTO after I left and went to Benetton. They continued to run GTO as a production facility, still making suspension and stuff.'

Meanwhile, as far as the racing was concerned, minor transmission problems beset the 640, but these were certainly not fundamental shortcomings. Hydraulic pump failures, broken wires to the electro-valves within the control system and other secondary glitches caused seemingly endless headaches for the first few European races. There was also a major vibration problem which took its toll on the V12 engine's alternator, but everything came right for the French Grand Prix from which point Mansell was never out of the top three right through to Spa, a run of success the highlight of which was a fine victory over Senna's McLaren-Honda at Budapest.

Barnard's departure from Ferrari meant he was unable to rekindle the partnership with Prost who, as it transpired, would accept an offer of around $6 million to join Ferrari in 1990 only two months after Maranello's announcement of the rift with the British designer.

Prost's relationship with McLaren had come to a head at the French Grand Prix in late June. Team chief Ron Dennis and TAG boss Mansour Ojjeh wanted a decision from the Frenchman as to his future plans. Speaking frankly, Prost conceded that he was unable to commit to staying with the team.

'This has not been an easy decision for me,' he admitted. 'Ron and Mansour wanted a prompt decision about next season and I was not comfortable about taking it at this stage. I have had a fabulous time with McLaren and we want to part with dignity – there will never be any problem between Alain Prost and the McLaren team.' The absence of any mention of his team-mate Ayrton Senna's name told its own story...

Meanwhile, if Prost was having problems with McLaren, Mansell found himself at war with the sport's governing body after an action-packed Portuguese GP. Nigel was leading commandingly when he made a stop for fresh tyres on lap 39 of the 71-lap race. But, in the excitement of the moment, he over-shot his pit and, rather than waiting for the Ferrari mechanics to pull him back into position, he selected reverse gear and backed up. It was a major breach of the regulations which would lead to his disqualification.

Mansell on the winner's rostrum at Estoril. Senna smiles confidently, knowing that his second place has enabled him to lengthen his championship points advantage over arch-rival Prost (LAT).

However, Mansell rejoined in third place and soon battled his way back onto the tail of Senna's second place McLaren. By lap 43, the stewards had advised Ferrari of Mansell's official disqualification and showed the black flag, together with Nigel's race number 27, at the start/finish line. Nigel, claiming he did not see the flag as he ran head-long down the straight into the setting sun, compounded his transgression by ramming into Senna under braking for the first corner, both cars spinning off at high speed into the gravel trap on the outside of that fast right-hander.

Gerhard Berger was left to run through to victory. After his 10 retirements in the first 11 races, this was a happy occasion for the Austrian. But it was irreversibly clouded by the Mansell controversy. Nigel left Estoril smarting under the impact of a $50,000 fine, but had absolutely no knowledge of the race stewards' decision to request that the sport's governing body suspend him from the following weekend's Spanish GP at Jerez.

Mansell countered the FIA's inability to convene a Court of Appeal before the Spanish race with a threat to retire from F1. It was not a strategy which had any effect whatsoever on the outcome of the governing body's deliberations. He was suspended from the Spanish GP and Ferrari President Piero Fusaro made clear his strenuous objections to FIA President Jean-Marie Balestre. Yet the drama passed, as all such motor racing dramas invariably do, and Mansell was back in harness in time for the Japanese GP at Suzuka.

Ferrari finished the season in third place behind McLaren and Williams in the Constructors' Championship. Yet Prost's recruitment for the 1990 season would prove to be one of the most electrifying for years, the Frenchman taking the Prancing Horse to within shouting distance of the World Championship before Ayrton Senna intervened to thwart his ambitions. At the same time, Mansell would become progressively

Prost with Fiat chief Gianni Agnelli. The Italian patriarch tried to make a point of keeping away from day-to-day Ferrari politics, but it wasn't always easy (LAT).

disaffected with his lot at Maranello and duly concluded that he wanted out. Berger had already gone, swapping places with Prost to partner Senna at McLaren.

On the design side, former McLaren engineer Steve Nichols would join Scalabroni on the technical staff as Chief Designer in November 1990. The quiet American immediately integrated himself into the Maranello operation with a degree of subtle tact and discretion, and set about the task of taking over responsibility for the development of John Barnard's type 640 concept. In fact, this was the second time in his professional career that Nichols had assumed such a challenge. In 1987 his McLaren MP4/3 was a studied evolution of Barnard's early TAG-powered design. Now he applied the same logical progression to the Ferrari 640 concept.

Yet again, the McLaren-Hondas were the cars at which to aim, so the basic specification of the new type 641 was not significantly changed for the 1990 season. The revised car had a fuel cell enlarged from 205 to 220 litres, a new diffuser panel, revised bodywork and a few aerodynamic modifications. The car was also significantly strengthened at the point where the hip-mounted side radiators attached to the chassis, in the light of Berger's shunt at Imola the previous year.

Prost's development input was extremely significant. The Frenchman made considerable progress to capitalise on the 640's reputation as a fine-handling chassis. The V12 engine all but matched Honda's rival V10 in top-end power, but was certainly lacking in low and medium-speed torque compared with the Japanese engine.

Everything seemed to go Alain's way once the 1990 season began. Thanks to Ayrton making a rare driving error at Interlagos, Prost took Ferrari to an immensely satisfying victory in the Brazilian's backyard. He followed that up with wins in Mexico, France and Britain. He finished the Silverstone race leading the Drivers' World Championship with 41 points to Senna's 29, leaving Mansell trailing in joint sixth on unlucky 13. This was more than the over-wrought Englishman could come to terms with, especially in his own backyard.

It was a cruel blow indeed. Mansell had qualified commandingly on pole position and, although Senna's McLaren took an early lead, Nigel was at the head of the field on lap 12. But even by that point, he knew his Ferrari was in deep trouble.

'On lap 10 my gearbox suddenly changed down from seventh to fourth on the straight,' he later explained. 'Apart from it being horrifyingly unpredictable, it was badly over-revving the engine and upsetting the car's balance under braking.'

Prost closed in relentlessly, but Nigel wasn't giving in without a fight. At one point, his wayward gearchange shifted from sixth to fourth in the middle of Stowe corner, then from seventh to first on the Hangar Straight. The Italian V12 was momentarily buzzed to 16,400rpm, but amazingly remained in one piece. Mansell had dropped behind Prost in second place when, with nine laps to go, the gearchange mechanism finally went haywire as he accelerated through Woodcote corner.

He pulled off on the exit to Copse corner and didn't even give Prost a glance as the Frenchman proceeded on his winning way. By the time he arrived back in the paddock, Mansell was simmering. 'Up to the point where I first experienced gearchange trouble, I was much quicker than anybody else,' he insisted. 'Obviously I'm very happy for Ferrari, but I'm bound to wonder why these things don't happen to the other guy.'

Within hours, Mansell decided – again – that he would retire from F1 at the end of the season and made public that announcement. At the start of the 1990 season he had been obliged to re-negotiate his contract to accommodate Prost as a team-mate of equal status. But now he was fast reaching the conclusion that the odds were being stacked against him. Years later, in his official autobiography, Mansell would accuse Ferrari of switching chassis so that Prost was always assured of the best equipment.

Although Ferrari team manager Cesare Fiorio urgently attempted to persuade Mansell to change his mind, Maranello went onto red alert. The obvious beneficiary of Nigel's announcement seemed to be Jean Alesi, in his first full F1 season. His performance with Tyrrell seemed to mark him out as an upcoming star. But the young French-Sicilian got himself so tangled up in complex contractual negotiations that he arrived at the very next race – Hockenheim – virtually tied up in knots.

In short Jean, whose early promise had generated considerable interest, seemed to have committed himself both to Williams and Ferrari for 1991, although nowhere near finalising a release from Ken Tyrrell, his existing employer. In fact, Alesi had signed a letter of intent with Ferrari plus a conditional contract with Frank Williams which would only become activated once he successfully concluded his negotiations to get out of his binding Tyrrell contract.

Meanwhile, Mansell seemed to be having a hard time sustaining his motivation. In the early stages of the German GP he had run close on Prost's heels in fourth place, the two Ferraris again playing second fiddle to the McLaren-Hondas of Senna and Berger. But while Alain would eventually scramble home a slightly disappointed fourth, Nigel ended his race in the pit lane garage.

Leaving the second chicane, he had drifted wide over the kerb and then understeered off across the grass at the exit of the fast Ostkurve. This left a front wing end-plate flapping disconsolately in the breeze, so Mansell just headed for the pits and retired. A Maranello spokesman was moved to remark, with considerable diplomacy, that perhaps Nigel may have concluded the car was more badly damaged than it actually was.

More disappointment followed at the Hungaroring. Prost's clutch seized, spinning him into retirement, while Mansell was taken out by the hard-charging Berger with only five laps to go while running third. Nigel emerged furious, his right wrist badly wrenched in an incident which moved Fiorio to call for an official inquiry by the sport's governing body. In retrospect, this was an enormous over-reaction to what had simply been the result of natural cut-and-thrust on an absurdly tight circuit.

Mansell couldn't do anything right, or so it seemed. At Spa he spun going into the first corner and the race was red-flagged to a halt. He took the spare Ferrari 641 for the restart, but was never happy with its handling. After 11 laps he came into the pits for a quick conference with Fiorio, briefly resumed and trailed round 15th before calling it a day. His dismal weekend was rounded off with a shouting match in the team's garage.

With a heavy-handed lack of tact, Ferrari waded in with some stern, if oblique criticism. 'After the car is examined, we will call Mansell in and have a very friendly, very frank talk and ask him for an explanation,' said a spokesman. It was hardly calculated to get the best out of Mansell going into the Italian GP at Monza where Prost and he finished second and fourth. Senna won and now led the Championship with 72 points to Prost's 56.

In the aftermath of these disappointing performances, it subsequently seems as though Ferrari took a good long look at Mansell's contract and pondered as to whether it was really worthwhile continuing with the Englishman on the team until the end of the year. Prost says he was told that Gianni Morbidelli might well replace Mansell in time for the Italian GP at Monza. But, for whatever reason, it never happened and Mansell – in Alain's words – was suddenly 'allowed to act in his own interests'. Nobody quite understood the meaning of this curious euphemism, although many people concluded that it had something to do with Mansell's subsequent behaviour in the Portuguese GP at Estoril.

By this stage in the season Maranello had certainly given up on the Mansell case. Now it was a matter of securing a replacement driver for 1991 and, after weeks of negotiations, it began to look as though Alesi would, after all, be staying on with Tyrrell. Consequently, Fiorio approached Benetton director Flavio Briatore to explore the possibility of recruiting the charismatic Alessandro Nannini. Terms were provisionally agreed, but when Nannini arrived to sign his deal, the offer on the table didn't quite tally with his understanding of the terms. Amazingly, this negotiating hiccup opened the door for Alesi to accept a Ferrari offer.

Frank Williams stood aside, his willingness smoothed by Ferrari's kind offer of a Ferrari 641 to join his own collection of historic Williams F1 racers at Didcot. Tyrrell completed the negotiations for Alesi's release and the contract was concluded.

Meanwhile, a seemingly revitalised Mansell qualified on pole at Estoril for the Portuguese GP. But when he veered across in front of team-mate Prost at the start, forcing the Frenchman to lose ground, Senna's McLaren got the jump on them both. Mansell eventually won ahead of Ayrton with a frustrated Prost third, the Frenchman convinced that Nigel had conspired with Senna to orchestrate this particular stunt.

Prost then whipped the gloves off. 'Ferrari doesn't deserve to be World Champion,' he said. 'It is a team without directive and without strategy trying to win against a well-structured team like McLaren. Berger helped Senna to the maximum to win the race.' This implied criticism of Fiorio's management abilities was later followed by a public endorsement of Alain's stance from Fiat boss Gianni Agnelli. Fiorio's position was certainly beginning to appear vulnerable, to say the least.

Nigel Mansell – affectionately known as 'Il Leone'. Many thought he had made an over-emotional decision to drive for Ferrari, but his technique at the wheel ensured that he was remembered as a classically heroic driver much to the taste of the Italian fans (LAT).

Prost with FIA Vice President Bernie Ecclestone (centre) and triple World Champion Niki Lauda. Both Alain and Niki learned a thing or two about Maranello politics during their respective careers (LAT).

Senna now led the World Championship by 18 points, but a week later that advantage had been halved thanks to Prost's victory in the Spanish GP at Jerez where Ayrton's McLaren retired with engine failure. Now the two men were nine points apart with two races, and 18 points, up for grabs. Mansell, who affected satisfaction with second place at Jerez, was chasing Berger for third place in the title.

In order to give Prost his best possible shot at the title, Ferrari went to the Japanese GP at Suzuka with a special qualifying chassis exclusively for the Frenchman's use. This incorporated a low-drag aerodynamic set-up for this very fast circuit near Nagoya. It included front wheel rim fairings and extensions to the rear body engine cover. Alain also tried a traction control system, but even so had to give best to Senna's McLaren in the battle for pole position.

Now it was Ayrton's turn to feel that the odds were stacked against him. To start with, he was dissatisfied that pole position was marked out on the dusty right-hand side of the start/finish straight. Even before qualifying began, Ayrton indicated that he would like it moved to the cleaner side of the track. Ironically, in the light of what was to follow, Alain concurred with his viewpoint. But the organisers declined to make any change.

Then, on race morning, it was declared that any driver running across the broken yellow line which separated the track proper from the entry lane to the pits would risk a penalty. Ayrton construed this as a direct reference to his overtaking lunge on Prost's sister McLaren the previous year when they had both collided and slid to a halt at the chicane. But this was the only place where one could seriously consider overtaking a closely matched competitor.

Senna mentally resolved that, if he was beaten to the draw by Prost at the start, his only option was to attempt sitting it out with the Ferrari going into the first high-speed right-hander. It was a risky strategy, but Senna was feeling distracted, hounded into a corner.

Alain was quickest in the warm-up. Ayrton's fears that the Ferrari was better in race trim looked well founded. Prost made the best start and sprinted for the first corner from the outside of the front row. But Ayrton aimed his McLaren down the inside and just kept on coming, slamming into the Ferrari with such an impact that the Italian car's rear wing was severed. The two cars hurtled into the gravel trap on the outside of the corner. But the organisers didn't deem it necessary to stop the race. Prost's title prospects had been wiped out at a stroke. Ayrton Senna was World Champion for the second time.

Alain was shaken to the core. He considered that Senna had simply driven him off the road, coldly and deliberately, in order to win the title. 'If everybody wants to drive in this way, then the sport is finished,' said Prost with understandable emotion.

'Senna is completely the opposite in character to what he wants people to believe. He is the opposite of honest. Motor racing is sport, not war. From a technical viewpoint, I believe we won the World Championship. Losing it this way is disgusting. We were not even side-by-side. If Senna's behaviour is to be expected, then we will perhaps get to a situation where people will start entering a team with one car specifically intended to push off the opposition to enable the other guy to win. This man has no value. I forget him...'

Senna, by the same token, blamed nobody but Prost. 'He took a chance going into the first corner when he couldn't afford to. He knew that I was going to come down the inside and he closed the door.' Neither man would ever agree with the other on this.

Fiat Vice-President Cesare Romiti hinted that Ferrari might consider quitting F1 in the wake of this controversy. 'We do not feel part of this world without rules,' he said. His views were expressed by Ferrari President Piero Fusaro who wrote to FISA President Balestre urging action to nip such driving tactics in the bud. The whole dispute was front page news for a couple of weeks, then gradually faded away.

Two weeks later, Senna crashed out of the Australian GP, leaving Mansell, who by now had reversed his retirement decision and done a deal to return to Williams, finishing second behind Nelson Piquet's Benetton-Ford, with Prost third. Ferrari thus ended the season with second place in the Constructors' Championship, 11 points behind the McLaren-Hondas.

It is tempting to conclude that the Suzuka affair effectively knocked the stuffing out of both Prost and Ferrari for the following year. Coming close enough to feel the taste of the victory champagne after a season which yielded five victories was a bitter let-down for the Frenchman. Not only did he feel aggrieved by Senna's behaviour, but he also suspected that Maranello hadn't really done enough consistently to underpin his own efforts throughout the season.

So it was perhaps no great surprise when 1991 saw Ferrari's F1 challenge become very seriously de-railed. With Maranello's unique mixture of misfound confidence allied to an ability to misjudge the calibre of the opposition, the team assumed that its late 1990 upsurge would be sustained into the following season. However, their calculations had failed to take into account both the force of the McLaren-Honda opposition, and the upcoming strength of the Nigel Mansell/Williams-Renault FW14 combination.

The result was a total disaster. Not only did the team fail to win a single race for the first season since 1986, but it was clear that Maranello's administrative structure was simply not up to the job. Rival teams watched in disbelief as petty feuding undermined Ferrari's entire F1 effort and Prost was driven from the organisation.

Prost was overtly critical of the way in which the Ferrari F1 programme had been permitted to lag behind. He'd said as much during the winter of 1990/91 and his frustration boiled over when the team was obliged to go into battle at the start of the new championship programme using what was essentially an up-rated version of the 1990 type 641. Small wonder both Alesi and Prost were blown away from the start, although Alain opened with a distant second place at Phoenix where the Italian V12 just didn't have the sheer power to match Honda's horses in a high downforce configuration.

Moreover, Prost found his relationship with team manager Cesare Fiorio difficult in the extreme. The former Lancia competitions boss had a personal profile almost as high, in some people's minds at least, as the drivers he controlled. Yet Prost did not believe he had a sufficiently sophisticated understanding of what was needed to win in the contemporary F1 environment. Factions began to develop within the team.

(It was not until the French Grand Prix, almost the season's half-distance point, that the new Ferrari 643 was ready for competitive action. This Steve Nichols design was essentially an evolutionary version of the previous year's Ferrari 642/2, with which it shared most of its running gear, but it was built round a totally new monocoque from the steering bulkhead forward. The undercut monocoque required the water radiators to be slightly repositioned further back along the car's flanks and the side pod tops were now incorporated integrally within a one-piece engine and cockpit cover. At Magny-Cours, Prost finished second after battling with Mansell's Williams FW14 during the opening stages, but the new Ferrari was bugged by high speed understeer and was at its best only in high downforce configuration.)

Meanwhile, on the management front there had been major changes. Just before the 1991 Canadian GP, the decision was taken to ditch Fiorio and introduce a fresh management structure into what was increasingly perceived as a rudderless F1 operation. Ferrari President Piero Fusaro, one of several Fiat nominees who had controlled the company in the aftermath of Enzo Ferrari's death in the summer of 1988, announced that the Commendatore's son Piero Lardi Ferrari would head up the team together with ex-Lancia engineer Claudio Lombardi and the highly experienced Marco Piccinini.

This looked cumbersome in the extreme and the questionable nature of the management was further put under the microscope when Fiat boss Gianni Agnelli's younger brother Umberto inexplicably made public his personal preference for Ayrton Senna. This was obviously calculated to make Prost see red, and although Ayrton allowed himself briefly to be romanced by the Prancing Horse, he ultimately knew which side his performance bread was buttered and signed again for McLaren into 1992.

It was perhaps no coincidence that Umberto Agnelli's intemperate comment came just as the Italian media was baying for Prost's blood. They had criticised him for failing to win on the Ferrari 643's debut in France, but Prost fought back and told them what he thought of the newspapers concerned. Unbelievably, instead of feeling sheepish and apologetic, the media demanded an explanation, an apology even. This inability to ignore what was written in the press was again proving to be one of the Ferrari management's most vulnerable shortcomings. Fusaro and his colleagues should of course have sided with Prost, but they were willing to be trampled over by the media. It was ever thus at Maranello.

Ferrari team manager Cesare Fiorio didn't hit it off with Prost professionally. By the summer of 1991 the former Lancia competitions boss had been replaced (LAT).

Yet Prost would not be intimidated. He was quite happy to tell Ferrari's management where it could get off. 'This is the last straw in a ridiculous sequence of events,' he insisted on race morning at Hockenheim. 'I don't think it is possible to resolve the problems I have with the press. They are always criticising me, giving me a lot of shit. It has turned out to be much more difficult than I ever thought. I suppose it was the same for John Barnard when he was working here, but I never imagined the influence of the press would be so considerable.'

Prost was also anxious about the 643's poor damping control in low downforce configuration, a trait which it had inherited from its predecessors. Steve Nichols was well aware of this problem and the engineering team secured the services of an ex-Showa shock absorber technician who had previously worked with Benetton in an effort to resolve the problem.

Nichols suspected the root of the problem to be aerodynamic, but the matter was not resolved by the end of the season. As the team's performance gradually faded, Prost became increasingly outspoken in his criticisms and eventually found himself fired after the penultimate race of the year for describing his Ferrari as 'a truck'.

On the Friday after finishing fourth at Suzuka, Prost was formally advised that his contract was being terminated. His lawyer was informed of this news by the Ferrari management and immediately telephoned Alain who was holidaying at Port Douglas, in Queensland, Australia. Even though it was clear that relations were deteriorating, Prost was stunned at the news.

Previous pages: In 1992 Ivan Capelli was to struggle to make his name with the troublesome F92A. Here he does his best to fend off Brundle's Benetton during the San Marino GP (LAT). Right: A touch of opposite lock for Jean Alesi also battling with the F92A (LAT).

Ferrari MD Claudio Lombardi seemed equally unsettled and embarrassed when he explained the situation at Adelaide where Gianni Morbidelli was signed to partner Alesi for the final race of the season. 'After deep analysis of Alain Prost's behaviour during the present season, we had to take the decision,' he said. 'We are always prepared to consider constructive criticism as a team, but Prost made too many critical comments outside the team.' There were also rumours of possible legal action from both parties.

'It is a shame that the season had to end like this,' said Alain. 'I had thought three weeks ago that we might have been able to reach a compromise which would have enabled me to stay at Ferrari. There was to have been a big change in the organisation. But Ferrari's treatment of me has been brutal. I am a free man now, I can do anything I want from now on.'

This off-the-cuff comment was followed up by a formal statement from the International Management Group which was responsible for Alain's business negotiations. It read: 'I confirm that Ferrari have terminated my contract and the matter is now in the hands of my lawyers.

'Whilst I regret that I should now be in a contentious situation with Ferrari as a result of what has occurred, I am relieved that what for me has been a very unsatisfactory season has been brought to an end. Despite my experiences this season, I retain my enthusiasm to drive in Formula 1 in 1992. In the light of possible litigation, I have been advised that I should not comment further at this point in time.'

For Alesi, this first season at Marenello ended with speculation that his contract might be sold off to another team. Many rivals now found themselves reflecting on his 1990 season with Tyrrell and wondering whether perhaps the nimble Cosworth V8-engined machine had flattered the Frenchman's talent. Certainly, his lack of experience initially meant he could contribute little to Maranello's overall test and development

programme, thus heaping even more responsibility onto Prost's shoulders.

The dismal season had ended with Ferrari taking third place behind McLaren and Williams in the Constructors' Championship. But there were key changes on the way which would suffuse even the most sceptical of observers with hope that Ferrari might be able to turn round its F1 operation. Even if it was beginning to look a little late in the day.

Chapter Two

Revival in sight

A matter of months separated the unceremonious departure of Alain Prost from the Ferrari ranks near the end of the 1991 season and the return of Luca Cordero di Montezemolo as Ferrari President (see panel page 136). His arrival could not make a material difference to the Ferrari team's F1 prospects for 1992, even though he sought to calm the overall mood by appointing triple World Champion Niki Lauda – whose 1975 and 1977 titles were won in a Ferrari – as advisor to the operation as well as, in effect, his own right hand man.

In many ways, this was seen as an attempt to revive the Dream Ticket of the mid-1970s, for Lauda was always ruthlessly pragmatic in his dealings within F1, never sparing anybody's feelings if he felt that mistakes were being made. By the same token, he was now deeply involved with the business expansion of his own thriving airline, LaudaAir, and there was no shortage of pit lane cynics who branded the new association as little more than a romantic trip down Memory Lane. The nostalgic element was reinforced by the appointment of 52-year old Sante Ghedini, another member of the 1970s Maranello operation, as team manager.

So why did Lauda need this sort of aggravation? In the paddock at Kyalami, prior to the first race of the season, he briskly explained his rationale to me for an interview which was published in *Autocar* a couple of weeks later.

'There are several factors to be considered,' he insisted. 'The first is that Ferrari, in my opinion, had an organisation which didn't work. Then it all changed with Montezemolo coming in. Suddenly there was an opportunity for me which hadn't been available before.

'My personal problem was that working seven days a week with aeroplanes meant I just didn't have any time left to think. But I come down here for three days, to a completely different scene, which is highly competitive and intense, and it serves as a major break for me. My role is purely to advise, to use my experience to assist. But I am not part of the team. I am just here to watch and say "look, why do it this way? Why not try that way?" But they can do whatever they want with the information.'

That seemed all right as far as it went. But Lauda appeared to have a very non-specific role, although he insisted that his lack of experience at the wheel of a contemporary F1 car was in no way a handicap. 'Communication is the key,' he insisted. 'You have to remember that at Ferrari this year there is a new group of people working together: [Chief Engineer] Harvey Postlethwaite, [aerodynamicist] Jean-Claude Migeot and Sante Ghedini. I am there as an interpreter between the team and the drivers, encouraging them to be more precise.'

He shrugged aside any prospect of potential aggravation with the Italian press. 'There

Luca di Montezemolo (right), now Ferrari President, discusses form with 'Mr Formula 1', Bernie Ecclestone at Buenos Aires, 1995. Between them is one-time Ferrari star Carlos Reutemann, now Governor of Argentina's Santa Fe province (LAT).

is no downside for me because I know the media and I know the problems,' he said confidently. 'So I make no comments to the media as far as the car's performance, day-to-day, is concerned. So if anybody asks me "how is the car going?" I just tell them to ask Claudio Lombardi. If I have an opinion, I tell him, not the press.'

Lauda also explained that his commitment to Ferrari was open-ended. 'The key point is that Montezemolo made clear my independent role from the outset. This wasn't easy to establish in the sense that, had I been given an official team position, it might have caused some jealousies. I don't want to get involved in the nitty-gritty details. I wanted a more general function and it took quite a while to get this established.'

At Kyalami, he stated, there were already signs of improvement in the way the team was operating. 'The calmness, organisation and cleanliness which exists at Ferrari this year is like day and night compared with some recent races I remember. I was amazed how much progress had been made when I arrived at Kyalami. It's certainly as good now as most British teams.'

Assuming this extremely optimistic assessment to be correct, what did Lauda really believe Ferrari could achieve in 1992? He immediately began to hedge.

'Ferrari's biggest problem is its past,' he replied. 'Now we are a completely new team we have to assess the value of the legacy, so it is important we take two or three races to establish precisely how well we are functioning. Then we will decide whether to make changes.

'Realistically, success for Ferrari cannot be expected before 1993, even if the current set-up is right, and the people are working in the right direction. So 1992 must be seen as a transitional year.' In that judgement, at least, Lauda was right on the button.

As far as the technical side was concerned, Ferrari had taken an ambitious approach with the aerodynamically complex F92A with its distinctive 'twin floor' configuration developed by Jean-Claude Migeot. The chassis engineering for this machine was outlined by Steve Nichols before he left the team just before Christmas 1991 in order to join the fledgeling Sauber F1 organisation. Harvey Postlethwaite, who had pioneered Ferrari's switch to carbon-fibre composite chassis construction in the early 1980s, then rejoined the team to find himself saddled with a car he freely confessed would not have been designed in this particular manner had he been in control of its technical conception from the outset.

Migeot had pioneered the distinctive high-nose aerodynamic concept with Tyrrell in 1990 and took the concept a step further with this new Ferrari. However, it differed significantly from the 1990 Tyrrell 019 arrangement on which a horizontal splitter beneath the car guided airflow from the nose into the radiator pods. On the Ferrari F92A, the side pods were raised about 15cm in order that this disturbed air could be channelled through open ducts to the rear diffuser. Thus the panel which formed the flat bottom undertray required by the F1 rules was effectively the lower level of a double floor configuration.

Wind tunnel results had initially seemed promising, but the F92A failed to match those optimistic expectations once it got out onto the circuit. In addition to its aerodynamic unpredictability, the Ferrari's progress was also blighted by a succession of oil system malfunctions which led to bottom end failures of the V12 engine. Furthermore, drivers Jean Alesi and his new Italian team-mate Ivan Capelli – who had joined from Leyton House – reported that the engines were basically gutless and unable to hold a candle to either the Renault or Honda V10s in pure performance terms.

Montezemolo in 1974, his first full season as Enzo Ferrari's right-hand man at the races. Together with Niki Lauda, he helped mastermind Ferrari's most consistently successful F1 run ever (LAT).

In the midst of all this chaos, Ferrari celebrated its 500th Grand Prix outing at Budapest in August 1992 and this was a race at which Luca di Montezemolo opted to make one of his rare appearances in an F1 paddock. He talked philosophically about the challenge involved in taking over Ferrari's presidency.

'I tell you this: for me, Ferrari is part of my life,' he said. 'I started my career with Ferrari and was lucky enough to be there at a successful time. Twice we won the championship, in 1975 and 1977, but this new challenge is very, very complicated.

'When I came back to Maranello, I found the situation in the racing department to be far worse than I had expected. Far worse. But we were lucky because we still have the specialised road car market to rely on and, even if the worldwide market is difficult, we are fortunate that our road cars are something very special, very different.'

Nevertheless, he did not in any way under-estimate the fact that Ferrari's F1 image remains central to the company's fortunes. 'In the racing department after I arrived last December, I spent five months working to understand the situation. I worked to understand the manpower, the potential of the car. Once I had absorbed all this I decided to approach the whole situation in a completely different manner. Ferrari had become an inflexible monolith of a company, which was not good for racing.

'I decided to divide it into three small departments: future developments in the UK under John Barnard (as Director of Research and Development); the engine department under Paolo Massai; and the Scuderia Ferrari under Harvey Postlethwaite, the place where we build the cars and from where we manage the team.'

The deal for Barnard to return to the Maranello fold, albeit operating another design out-station in Britain, had been completed barely six weeks earlier. 'I am very happy to have reached an agreement with John because, even for him, this is a huge opportunity.

'I also want to build up a strong relationship between our UK facility and Italy in order to take full advantage of the F1 silicon valley in England for chassis development and specialist sub-contractors, while still harnessing the huge potential of Maranello.'

Inevitably critics immediately responded by asking Montezemolo precisely how he intended to avoid the problems involved in running GTO, the previous Ferrari UK-based design operation which had been scaled down when Barnard left in 1989 to join Benetton?

'I will tell you my viewpoint very clearly,' he responded. 'I think that the GTO concept of Enzo Ferrari was a super idea. Unfortunately, at the time Ferrari was very old and the situation was managed in a very bad way. But the fundamental idea was very good.

'For me, the approach is slightly different. First of all, I am in charge of the company with full powers, so I can take a decision without anybody else taking a parallel initiative. I take my responsibilities and I want the people in the company to follow my ideas. If they follow, I am very happy. If they don't, then there are many other doors, many possibilities available to them outside Ferrari.' In other words, they can put up or shut up.

He continued the theme: 'My objective is to create a smaller racing department which contains less bureaucracy. Of course, there will be a lot of discussion between the engine and chassis departments. In Maranello we have a huge organisation geared to building cars, but I want to take advantage of the UK facilities and, for a world-wide company like Ferrari, it is certainly not a scandal to have an affiliate in the UK.

'If you want to make pasta, then you have to be in Parma. I want to make a sophisticated F1 project, so I want to be involved in England. Then it is up to me to put everything together.

'It is a big challenge for all of us: for John Barnard, to get back to the winners' rostrum, and for Ferrari to regain its competitiveness and solve its problems. This could be a good way.'

Barnard meanwhile was assessing his new challenge. 'Towards the end of 1991 I was approached by Montezemolo with the offer of going to Ferrari, in Maranello, as Technical Director,' he recalls. 'I declined the offer again because of my fundamental reservations of not moving away from here, having a young family and not wanting to be away for a month at a time, or whatever it would have had to be to work in Maranello.

'Then they did the deal with Harvey who went back to Maranello again at the end of 1991. Then come July 1992, Niki Lauda approached me and said Ferrari was discussing the possibility of setting up another base in England, was I interested?

'Well, at that time I'd been working with TOMs, up in Norfolk, together with a lot of members of my group from before, and started to set it up with the idea of going into Formula 1. The idea was a Toyota-engined car, to start to work on something and hopefully suck Toyota in before the project ran out of steam, if you like. So we set about finishing off the factory. It wasn't a big one, but it was quite nicely kitted out with drawing office, computers, autoclaves [giant ovens for 'baking' carbon fibre components to give them their final strength] were ordered, and so on. Unfortunately it ran out of steam before any serious money could be attracted.

'So then Ferrari started talking to me again. I'd had a bad experience with Benetton; there were some things I understood were signed and sealed which didn't quite happen, so I was very bitter and twisted about it.

'At that stage I thought, well, I'd always had a hankering to get back to do my own team again, or at least to be a major partner like I used to be with Ron in the early days, and that's what I'd thought the Benetton situation would do for me. So when that all went belly-up, I then turned and started thinking "at least with a big company like Ferrari, although you're working for someone else and there are all the consequent problems, at least (a) I know the problems and (b) I think they're going to be in racing as long as I am and the money will be there". So from the security aspect I decided to go back to Ferrari.'

In 1992, Alesi found himself elevated to team leader following the departure of Alain Prost. But his confidence was dented when the F92A turned out to be a machine whose good looks were not backed up by on-track performance (Allsport).

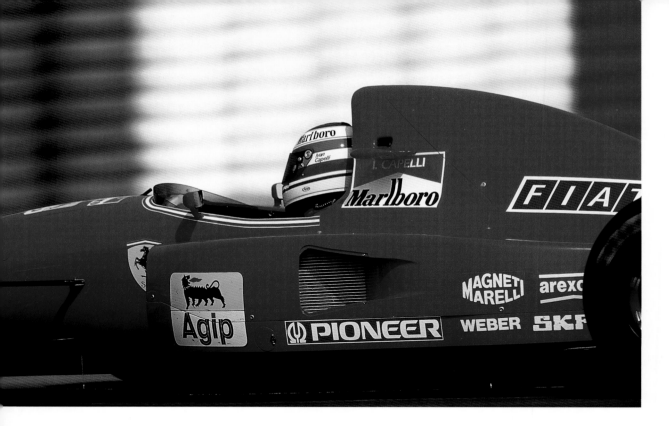

Previous pages and above: Alesi's team-mate from the start of 1992 was the highly-rated Ivan Capelli, seen here at the San Marino GP. Sadly, as with so many previous Italian drivers at Maranello, the cards fell against him and he was left wrestling with an uncompetitive car (LAT).

Such was the Italian company's enthusiasm to have Barnard based at Maranello that they even offered to collect him in a Fiat private jet on Monday mornings from the Dunsfold aerodrome, close to his Surrey home, and deliver him back there on Friday evening. But John still wasn't interested, preferring to stay close to his family.

'We did the deal and started setting up the place in England again, which was a bit annoying, having seen Ferrari get rid of the old GTO set-up six months before that. This (Northfield House) was available, so we grabbed it with the intention of only being here for a short time because they were already saying "can you get on and design next year's car?"

'And I mean, this is the problem. You don't just walk into an office, snap your fingers and say "get me a drawing board, get me a computer, get me a secretary – right, now we'll sit down and design a car". It doesn't work like that.'

Back in the thick of the F1 action, Ferrari was finding that not much worked at all in 1992. By the time the season came to an end in Adelaide, the F92A had earned a reputation for giving its drivers a punishing, lurching ride over the bumps as well as delivering a pathetic power output, estimated in some circles as between 70 and 100bhp down on the championship-winning Renault V10.

I tracked down Niki Lauda and asked him if his predictions hadn't gone badly wrong? 'We have spent this season learning precisely where we are,' he replied firmly. 'We can now face a 1993 season of serious transition out of total chaos into something better. That is as much as I can guarantee, because we now have a base from which to start working.'

Surely, though, the harsh reality was becoming clear that Maranello didn't have a serious grasp of what was involved in fielding a competitive F1 car for the 1990s? Lauda rejected the criticism. 'I hope I have helped to make them realise what's needed,' he said. 'But the engine department is an area where I have still not got the full solution to the problem, but we are working on it and it's getting better and better.'

However, there was no denying that Ferrari also had problems on the driver front. Ivan Capelli's F1 career had effectively stalled after the disappointments of the season, while Jean Alesi's position seemed on the point of being threatened by the news that Gerhard Berger was returning to the Ferrari fold for 1993 after three seasons at the wheel of a McLaren-Honda. So did Lauda feel that Berger was set to receive preferential treatment? And did he agree that Alesi's position was becoming vulnerable?

'The driver contracts for 1993 simply state that both drivers will get the same technical back-up,' he said. 'He (Gerhard) has in his contract, for example, that if there is only one of a certain type of wing available, he has the first choice. My feeling is to always give them the same equipment, because you don't really need two drivers if you're only going to support one.' That was as maybe, but Lauda did concede that Gerhard's deal stipulated priority access to the spare car. Alesi's position, whichever way Maranello tried to slice it, was being significantly undermined.

So was Jean happy about it? Lauda picked his words with care. 'It's normal in life that in these situations, when the new guy comes in, he tries to negotiate a deal where he gets the best. But we've sorted that out now. There is no problem. Alesi is happy; I had to explain to him the way it's going to be and now it is clear. We will bring four cars as often as we can, but he will have no problems with access to the spare car.'

Again, I posed Lauda essentially the same question I put to Montezemolo four months earlier. Why did he think a UK-based design studio would create a politically less volatile situation than it had done last time round with GTO? And would Barnard's role as Director of Research and Development be confined to just that?

'Yes, all the design (information) will be brought to Italy where it (the car) will be built under Harvey Postlethwaite's authority. Nothing will be built in England. Previously the arrangement didn't work because Harvey and John were working against each other.

'The set-up (with GTO) was wrong. This time, the logical approach is to make sure there is no conflict between them. But John working on his own doesn't do Ferrari any good if there isn't a counterpart in Italy who speaks Italian and English to ensure that there is good communication between the two centres. So thank goodness we have got Harvey into a position where he agreed to run Italy and communicate backwards and forwards with England.'

As far as 1993 was concerned, Lauda was upbeat about the team's prospects. 'The car that will be in South Africa (at the start of 1993) is a Barnard car and there will be another Barnard car for Magny-Cours (mid-season). John is responsible for both cars next year – there is no more political who-does-what.'

Whether he was attempting to talk-up Maranello's future prospects or simply biting his tongue to sound manifestly over-optimistic is not really clear. Either way, the 1993 season certainly did not unfold to the agenda he predicted.

Ferrari's efforts were seriously clouded by the continuing uncertainty over the future F1 technical regulations. The team's stop-go strategy on the subject of an active suspension development cost Maranello dearly. In order to make up time, Barnard worked flat out to design a system in less than two months. Inevitably, there were teething problems.

Barnard explains: 'As far as the 1993 car was concerned, it was kind of a revised chassis based on the previous year's twin-floor car. I did get involved in that, but obviously not enough to steer it fundamentally, so the idea of this building was to enable us to get going quickly.

'I was able to pull in a lot of my old group, which meant that things could happen fairly quickly with people knowing what to do without being spoon-fed, which was important. The group included Peter Brown (Composites), Graham Saunders (Machine Shop), Brian Pepper (Fabrication), Andy Smith (Materials and Testing), the stress guys, Mark Stevens, Nick Chapman, and ultimately Mike Coughlan, and plenty of other blokes who'd been with me for years. This basic group had been with me through GTO and Benetton and now were back with Ferrari again.

'The specialist workforce is all based in this geographic area, so any move to Norfolk (to TOMs) would have been a major step. I actually sat with a number of these people and said "look, if this came up, what would you think about it?" and they were mostly prepared to have a go up there. But it would have been much better if they hadn't had that decision to make.'

For the F93A design, Barnard and the rest of the Maranello design team had made the decision to commit to an active system in preparation for 1994. But they had reckoned without the rule makers who decided to ban active suspension from the end of 1993, although the decision was not finally set in stone until the German GP that August.

For the opening race of the 1993 season at Kyalami, both cars were equipped with Barnard's original active ride system. Alesi's had coil springs and Berger's gas struts as its spring medium. From the word go there were problems with the software control system which had to be addressed, but Gerhard in particular went into the season with extreme reservations about the F93A's handling.

The Austrian's first pre-season test with the car at Estoril had proved to be a miserable business. He never felt comfortable in the car and was unnerved by the lack of progressive feel which all drivers regarded as a key element in the functioning of such systems. As a result, it didn't take long for his driving style to become tinged with a touch of desperation.

John Barnard chats with his former partner, McLaren International boss Ron Dennis (LAT).

Sole F1 pioneer fights on

Motor racing statistics can be notoriously misleading barometers of fact, yet what is indisputable is that Ferrari stands alone as the sole survivor of the World Championship pioneers, the only team still competing which was in at the birth of the official title contest in 1950.

In the summer of 1951, Froilan Gonzalez's superb victory in the British GP at Silverstone with the 4.5-litre unsupercharged type 375 had put Ferrari on the Grand Prix winning map for the first time. Thereafter, Maranello's rise through the ranks came as little surprise at a time when Italy was synonymous with Formula 1 success.

By the end of 1951, Alfa Romeo had notched up a total of 10 Grand Prix wins with its legendary, supercharged 158s and 159s. Yet thanks to Ferrari's dominance of the 1952 and 1953 World Championships, run under F2 regulations due to dire shortage of fully-fledged contemporary Formula 1 cars, Maranello vaulted to the head of the winners' table with 17 wins by the end of 1953.

From that point onwards, Ferrari remained something of a Formula 1 yardstick throughout the 1950s and early 1960s. By the end of 1961, the marque had posted a total of 35 Grand Prix victories in 12 seasons. The closest challenger was Cooper, by then on 16, but with their glory days beginning to fade.

There were no wins for Ferrari in 1962 and just a single success – John Surtees's maiden GP victory at Nurburgring – in 1963 to bring the total to 36. By now F1 had entered the golden era of Colin Chapman and Lotus, the British constructor confidently reeling off the wins to complete the 1970 season with 42 victories. But Ferrari, despite only intermittent success, was still ahead with 46.

The crossover point came in the 1973 Spanish Grand Prix at Barcelona's Montjuich Park circuit. Despite struggling with a slowly deflating rear tyre in the closing stages of the race, reigning World Champion Emerson Fittipaldi just managed to squeeze home the winner. It was Lotus's 50th Grand Prix victory, topping Ferrari's total of 49 and moving into the lead of the all-time winners' stakes at long last.

At the end of 1973, Lotus had expanded its advantage to 54 wins, and 57 at the end of the following season. But by then Maranello was on the verge of the most convincing resurgence in its history. Between the start of 1974 and the end of 1979, Ferrari won no fewer than 30 Grands Prix, three drivers' championships and four constructors' titles. Lotus never got a sniff of the Italian cars again, from a statistical standpoint at least.

Thereafter, stringing together consistent success proved extraordinarily elusive for Ferrari. Strangely so, one might be tempted to suggest.

He opened the season with a fortuitous sixth place in South Africa, but then tangled spectacularly with Michael Andretti's McLaren as the pack accelerated away from the start of the Brazilian GP at Interlagos. The McLaren and Ferrari, locked together, careered off the circuit on the approach to the first corner, Andretti's machine flying over the wayward Ferrari after the initial impact, smashing into the Italian car's rollover bar and passing uncomfortably close to Gerhard's head. 'I just don't understand how something like this can happen,' fumed Berger. 'Andretti moved so violently I had no time to react. I couldn't move out of the way and I couldn't brake.'

Alesi finished a disappointing eighth, having lost ground with two stop-go penalties, and the Maranello twosome's season continued in a miserable vein when it came to the rain-soaked European GP at Donington, where both cars dropped out with leaks from the hydraulic active control system.

Not until the Monaco GP, round six of the Championship, did Ferrari register a podium finish, with Alesi following Ayrton Senna's McLaren-Ford and Damon Hill's Williams-Renault home in third, despite a badly overheating V12 for much of the race. Gerhard collided with Hill at the Loews hairpin, making an over-exuberant bid to take

Berger looks pensive before the start of the 1993 European GP. It was a bad day as he retired with a leaking hydraulic active control system (LAT).

second place in the closing stages of the race. Damon managed to continue, but Berger was out on the spot with broken right front suspension.

So the season ground on relentlessly. Berger was a distant fourth at Montreal, neither car managed to score points in the French GP, and only Alesi survived to a lonely ninth at Silverstone where active suspension problems again sidelined Berger. It was half-way through the season and Ferrari had only nine Constructors' Championship points in the bank as compared with the Williams team's 95. It was a desperate situation.

For the first few races it had been a question of experimentation with the active system and attempting to learn about its intricacies as quickly as possible.

'The Spanish GP really established the need for us to make major changes to the system,' recalled Barnard. 'Up to then we had been trying to overcome some of our problems by running over-stiff dampers, but the high-frequency bumps at Barcelona really caught us out and we had a horrific time. After that we designed a co-axial system with hydraulic spring platforms with the damping control linked to the pushrods.'

With no facility to equip the F93A with mechanical anti-roll bars, the team had to persevere with electronic roll control from the start and this element in the equation continued to prove enormously frustrating. John recalls that the system 'got in a bit of a knot' at around the time of the French GP where, in addition, the team was coming to grips with a revised aerodynamic package, including nose section, underbody section and new front wings.

'We were not really sure which area to attack first,' he explained, 'so we just battled through Magny-Cours and Silverstone, both bad races for us, before getting the software system sorted out a bit for Hockenheim.

'We then decided to have a look at the possibility of building a car incorporating rocker arms which would enable us to use a mechanical anti-roll bar as well as examining the prospects for passive suspension for 1994. But in the end, for racing purposes, we continued to develop the co-axial system and although we built a chassis with rocker arms, it was only used for testing and never raced.'

The month of June saw another fresh face joining the Ferrari management structure in the form of ex-Peugeot competitions manager Jean Todt, fresh from masterminding the French team's second straight Le Mans triumph. In his role of Sporting Director, Todt was charged with doing for Ferrari's race organisation what Barnard was attempting to do on the technical side.

Todt realised it was going to be a long job. Rather than impetuously trying to impose any dramatic changes, he kept a low profile for the first few months of his new employment, watching, noting and assessing what needed to be changed at Maranello in the longer run. He first appeared in the pit lane at the German GP, a weekend on which he also experienced something of a baptism of fire at a Constructors' Association meeting designed to thrash out the technical regulations for 1994.

Hockenheim was not an easy event. Berger may well have been one of the highest paid F1 drivers of the 1993 season, reputedly having returned to Maranello for a $10 million fee, but all the money in the world could not compensate for the sheer frustration he was experiencing. At Hockenheim, Gerhard and Jean finished sixth and seventh, Berger having earlier tried to edge Mark Blundell's Ligier-Renault onto the grass at around 190mph.

'What Gerhard did might have been acceptable in the last couple of laps in a race,' said a shaken Blundell, 'but not at half distance. I shall be having a quiet word about it with him when I next see him. He certainly had some extra-wide wheels on his Ferrari...'

After a morale-boosting third at Hungaroring, Gerhard found himself in more trouble with Blundell when the two cars again collided at Spa, this time while battling for a

Harvey Postlethwaite chats to Berger in the pit lane at the 1993 Monaco GP (LAT).

lowly tenth place. 'Although my wheels were level with the middle of his car, he chopped into me and pitched me up onto two wheels,' seethed the beleaguered Englishman. 'By a miracle I didn't turn over, but then the car hit a guard rail. When he got out of his car he told me that he knew I would attack at that point, because I was quicker, but that fighting for tenth place was only a game!'

However, Gerhard had a different view of the proceedings. 'I looked in my mirror and saw that he was nowhere near enough to try overtaking – then the next thing I knew he was coming over the top of me.' Alesi, meanwhile, had retired early with handling problems.

Barnard's own frustration had started to boil over by now. 'I'm not enjoying myself,' he admitted to *Autosport* in early August. 'We are sweating blood at a time we ought to be concentrating on a new car. We are being pounded to get results because, three years ago, Ferrari let the ball slip and dropped the active suspension system it was working on. Other people plugged on and have gone through the pain we are now having, out of the public eye. We are having to do it in the middle of the racing season. Ferrari is always in the public eye so when you have a problem like this, it is 100 times worse for us.

'At the end of last year we thought active was going to carry on and we took the decision to make a car which was committed to having active suspension. We thought we could solve it, but the problem of electronic roll control has proved to be much more difficult than anybody ever thought.

'There is also a certain temperament at Ferrari which is different from the British one-foot-in-front-of-the-other approach, where you slog along, with a stream of oaths or whatever, and you get there in the end.'

Most of his frustration was reserved for the F1 rule makers. 'We seem to be going into a flat spin and I can't really remember a situation like it, where we have been so uncertain for so long. I remember in the past when we complained of things being forced upon us with no notice, like flat bottoms and so on, but this one has gone on and on. I

Former Peugeot competitions chief Jean Todt joined Ferrari as Sporting Director in 1993 (LAT).

thought I could follow what was going on up until the World Council meeting in Paris after the British GP. After that, I am afraid I completely lost the ball.

'What we seem to have ended up with is a status quo for the end of this year with active suspension out for next year, but gearboxes staying as they are. By that I take it they mean fully automatic gearboxes, because we are now running fully automatic upshift mechanisms.'

Then came Monza, an event which could oh-so-easily have ended in a total catastrophe for the Ferrari team. Buoyed up after a programme of intensive pre-race testing at the famous Milanese circuit, Alesi predicted that the Prancing Horse had a chance of winning at home. It was just the sort of heady assertion calculated to throw the fans into a frenzied state of high octane emotion. Yet the two Ferrari drivers very nearly failed to survive even qualifying.

Having set Saturday's third fastest qualifying time behind the Williams FW15Cs of Alain Prost and Damon Hill, Jean eased up and was cruising back to the pits when he was lured into a potentially fatal misunderstanding with Berger. Gerhard had missed the chequered flag and was still running flat out on what should have been his slowing down lap, when he came upon Alesi coming into the Variante Ascari S-bend.

Jean saw the other Ferrari coming up in his mirrors and moved to the left, intending to concede the racing line to his faster-moving colleague. Unfortunately, Berger had moved in the same direction a split-second earlier. The Austrian found himself faced with the rear end of Alesi's machine, braked furiously and immediately lost control. The Ferrari slammed into the guard rail on the left before hurtling back across the track, skimming over the gravel trap and sideways into the protective tyre barrier on the right. Mercifully, he escaped without injury and was happy to settle for an official reprimand from the stewards as his sole legacy of what had been a chilling episode.

In the race, with Hill and Senna losing time after a first corner collision, Alesi was able to jump into an immediate second place at the start, completing the opening lap 1.7sec behind Prost's Williams. He would finish the afternoon in the same position, but behind Hill's Williams after Prost's Renault V10 expired with only five of the race's 53 laps left to run. Berger retired after 15 laps with a loose sensor in the active suspension system.

A Ferrari finishing second was one thing, but a Ferrari leading a race was quite another. Alesi managed to achieve that latter, recently rare, feat by heading the field for the first 19 laps of the Portuguese GP at Estoril, eventually fading to finish fourth behind Michael Schumacher's Benetton-Ford, Prost and Hill.

This particular event was made memorable by another close shave which set Berger's heart racing a lot faster than the red cars had managed so far this season. Accelerating back into the fray following a scheduled tyre stop at the end of lap 35, he found that the active suspension developed a mind of its own over a bump at the end of the pit lane.

The Ferrari turned sharp left and plunged straight across the circuit into the left-hand barriers. Derek Warwick's passing Footwork-Mugen only missed T-boning the errant Italian machine at 175mph by literally a couple of feet. It had been potentially the most serious accident in F1 history.

Neither Ferrari finished the Japanese GP at Suzuka, but fourth and fifth in the Australian GP was just sufficient for the team to retain fourth place in the final Constructors' Championship order behind Williams, McLaren and Benetton.

At the end of 1993, Harvey Postlethwaite had completed his two-year contract with Ferrari and decided to leave. From a pure contractual standpoint, the British engineer had found Maranello extremely straightforward to work with, but he was edging towards the conclusion that the operational infrastructure of the F1 team was such that

Gerhard Berger leans into Parabolica during the Italian GP at Monza. No luck on this day, either (LAT).

Ferrari was never going to be able to string together more than a fleeting degree of sustained success.

'I was beginning to find the whole thing a little too cumbersome for my taste,' he admitted. 'I'd had some good times with Ferrari, especially first time round when the Old Man was alive, but by the end I had too many memories of sitting in planning meetings with about 40 other people, all talking, all getting nowhere.'

Postlethwaite was also aware of an inflexibility at Maranello which tended to conspire against making changes in the racing department's workforce if that was deemed necessary. There were situations where he could see that certain employees needed to be moved – or even fired – but the bureaucratic approach of the personnel department often blocked such key staff changes. 'By the time I left, I had reached the conclusion that Ferrari might recover to the point that they might win races, or even a World Championship. But I could never see them stringing it together long enough to win two Championships – and five years down the line they might well be back to square one.'

Postlethwaite's departure meant that Barnard was now left totally in charge of the technical side of the F1 operation while Jean Todt's calming presence was brought to bear on the immediate challenge of operating the cars in the field. Going into 1994, it was now over three years since Ferrari had last won a World Championship Grand Prix.

The clock was ticking away. At Maranello there was pressure from Fiat, from the media, from everybody from Montezemolo downwards. They wanted Barnard to produce results. Yet the English engineer had barely reached one-third distance in his three-year plan for a Ferrari revival. They would have to wait yet awhile.

Chapter Three

Designing the new cars

But what of the cars being created to bring about Ferrari's renaissance, and the man behind their design? And what made John Barnard, appointed Director of Research and Development in the summer of 1992, think that things at FDD (Ferrari Design & Development) would be significantly different from at GTO, Ferrari's previous UK-based design operation that had been run down when he left to join Benetton three years earlier? 'Well,' he laughs, 'it was basically the same this time. Niki Lauda said that Ferrari wanted to do something in England again, and was I interested, but fundamentally I think it was a way of getting me on board.

'Now, whether they thought – given a year or two – they could squeeze me across to Maranello, I don't know. Whether they thought they could get me to operate with an office and a secretary from here and act as a full-time running consultant at Maranello, I don't know. But that was never discussed, and it was never my intention. So here we are and here we stay.

'My experience from the first time round at GTO taught me that I cannot run the F1 operation at Maranello on a day-to-day basis from England, and that's what I told them from the outset. I told them if they wanted something in England, the best way I know of making it work is having a virtually stand-alone set-up which can work on the design and development of a new car. In other words, we have to work ahead of the racing programme, which meant, this time round, I needed the production facilities I had before because you need a certain amount of physical capability in order to push forward with design.

'You can't just design everything new on a piece of paper without making some test pieces or carrying out static tests, or some kind of prior investigation first to know what you want to design is a possibility. So you have to have that facility.

'The other thing we have this time at FDD, which we didn't have at GTO, is our own aerodynamics department – and that was fundamental to doing a new car. Last time it was all done in Maranello, and I know, from my own experience, I have to have a good tunnel and people who will analyse the numbers and work on the car's aerodynamic development the way I want to go. This is important because there are a lot of ways you can work in that area; in ways of interpreting the numbers, what areas you consider to be important versus what somebody else considers to be important, you can create quite a different package.

'Ultimately, I have certain beliefs about certain aspects of the car. You could sit down with half a dozen experts and argue for six months whether one way was a better way rather than another, but the bottom line is that this is my job. I make that decision and that's the way it's going to go.

'I don't want to have a situation where I have a belief about the way I want the car

John Barnard, long regarded as an audacious and imaginative engineer (LAT).

to be, and then see somebody else in another place developing it off in another direction which I think is wrong. And if that happens, then I'll go. Basically, I'm right or I'm wrong. But I'm also in charge, so it was very important to have that aerodynamic facility.'

The challenge of establishing a bespoke aerodynamic programme was one of John's first priorities when he established FDD at Northfield House, Shalford. Ironically, he now occupied the building alongside the former GTO premises which had been sold off to McLaren Cars as a manufacturing unit for carbon-fibre composite chassis components used in the BMW-engined F1 super performance road coupé. But road cars were far from Barnard's mind as he began to focus on picking up the threads of his Maranello relationship.

'There is a wind tunnel on site at Ferrari Racing,' he explained. 'This was being built when I went there at the end of 1986. It was operational some time early 1987-ish and, again, there was a little bit I could bring in terms of the set-up from what I'd done in this connection at McLaren.

'That is to say, it was a one-third scale model – the same as we had been using at McLaren – and at that time it was as good as there was out there. But like all these things, your facilities have to keep developing with the car, and that didn't happen (in this case). If you looked at it when I came back this time, I had got to the point of being at Benetton – seeing what they'd got, laughed at it and went about setting up a new facility in terms of the Farnborough facility (at the Royal Aircraft Establishment).'

A corresponding step forward had not

The most visually distinctive aspect of the Ferrari F92A was its elliptical ducting to the water radiators. This trend was duplicated – albeit to better effect – on the John Barnard F310 for Michael Schumacher to drive in 1996 (LAT).

Ivan Capelli's F92A stands in the pit lane garage minus its wheels, showing off the dramatic side pod treatment to striking effect (LAT).

taken place at Ferrari. The tunnel was effectively the one being used in 1986/87. It wasn't up to the job. Barnard: 'We therefore had to sort out what tunnel we were going to use. I wanted to get back into the Farnborough tunnel, but I was kept out politically. Benetton managed to close the door on us.

'We then had to go and find somewhere suitable, and there aren't that many tunnels around which fitted the bill. But when we had been looking around for Benetton, before we went to Farnborough, one of the tunnels we did look at was the one owned by British Aerospace down in Bristol, but at that time it was a much more difficult exercise to convert it into having a rolling road than it would have been at Farnborough.

'However, British Aerospace's aircraft work was dropping off and this time they came and approached us. We said well, we were interested and, although it was quite an effort installing the rolling road, ultimately I think it's a better tunnel. It's a bit bigger, catering for 50 per cent models; and because we'd been through the exercise in building rolling roads on two previous occasions, we had a fair handle on it. Now there are some more technical facilities and it has been fully functioning, running smoothly and beneficially since about the start of 1995.'

Chassis design sluggish in 1960s

Although Italy may have been the epicentre of international motor racing throughout the 1950s, the emergence of Cooper and Lotus as Formula 1 forces shifted the focus of Grand Prix engineering to Great Britain. By the early 1960s, it was clear that UK-based teams had a virtual monopoly on both chassis and engine technology, eclipsing the early advantage displayed by Ferrari in 1961, the first season to be run under the 1.5-litre engine regulations.

In simple terms, Enzo Ferrari had always tended to be an engine man. Throughout the 1950s, Maranello's power units had been regarded as the heart of the team's technical equation. Chassis engineering seemed to take an often poor second place, but this would not be good enough as the 1960s developed.

Increasingly, Colin Chapman, John Cooper – and later both Jack Brabham and Bruce McLaren – raised the stakes by understanding that the key to future success was integrating the engine and chassis into one cohesive unit. Nobody had a sharper appreciation of this reality than Chapman. In 1967, the introduction of the sensational new Cosworth Ford DFV-engined Lotus 49 would, in terms of pure performance, render obsolete not only Ferrari, but the entire opposition in the Grand Prix field.

As far as Ferrari was concerned, it remained out on a technical and geographic limb for much of the 1960s. Recruiting former motorcycle World Champion John Surtees as a driver at the start of 1963 seemed like a very positive move: the Englishman brought with him much knowledge of British chassis design trends thanks to his two F1 seasons with the Reg Parnell and Yeoman Credit Lola teams.

Yet although he worked well with Mauro Forghieri, Ferrari's bright up-and-coming F1 engineer, Surtees eventually fell foul of Maranello's complex politics. He was too outspoken for many of those who had Enzo Ferrari's ear. In 1966, after the Scuderia unveiled its new V12-engined challenger for the new 3-litre formula, Ferrari's team manager Eugenio Dragoni figured he could do without Surtees on the books.

After a confrontation with the Englishman, based on the inaccurate premise that John was not fully recovered from injuries sustained when he crashed his Can-Am Lola sports car the previous autumn, Dragoni was well satisfied when Surtees quit the team on the eve of the Le Mans 24-hour race. However, the assumption that Ferrari's technical equipment was now sufficiently competitive to render lesser drivers, including Dragoni's protege Lorenzo Bandini, capable of winning races was to prove uncomfortably wide of the mark.

Throughout the second half of the 1960s, Ferrari enjoyed some competitive showings, but only managed to score a single Grand Prix victory between Monza in 1966 and Austria in 1970. This success was Jacky Ickx's memorable triumph in the 1968 French GP, yet no wins came the way of the brilliantly talented New Zealander Chris Amon who drove for the team for three years from the start of 1967.

Amon's luck was as unfortunate as his judgement in picking teams, so it was perhaps no surprise that when he decided to leave Maranello and join the fledgeling works March team in 1970, Ferrari mounted another convincing revival which saw them come close to a World Championship with the elegant flat-12 engined 312B1. However, at the end of the day it was Jochen Rindt who won the drivers' title for Lotus, albeit posthumously.

Of course, the need for a new wind tunnel was simply one facet within the wider perspective of John Barnard's commitment to a three-year plan designed to return Ferrari to a state of F1 competitiveness. The formula had worked first time round with the Italian team, then paid off again at Benetton. But there would inevitably be a degree of impatience emanating from Maranello, an understandable desire for events to progress quicker than was realistically possible.

Barnard shakes his head knowingly: 'You can go in. I've sat and said it will take three years. We've got to spend this and that. OK, they say, so give us a bottom line figure. So I do. Six months later it's sometimes as if you hadn't opened your mouth. They have difficulty conceiving long-term plans in F1. They agree, and nod their head, but in the back of their mind they would like to win three or four races the following year. As soon as you get to the first race, they're looking at the chequered flag and saying "where are we?"

'You just have to close your eyes and bulldoze ahead. 1993, complicated by the active, was one of the most difficult seasons I'd ever had. In the back of my mind I'm thinking that we're just passing through on the way to the terminus. I'm looking out of the window, it's all going past in a blur and I can't do anything about it because I can't stop the train and get off at that station because I don't want to be at that station. I want to be at the end of the line.'

In 1994, Ferrari really began to see first signs of the Barnard involvement paying off. The high-nose 412T1 showed itself to be a pretty competitive car on several occasions, but John's efforts to get the best out of it were thwarted by problems with the Maranello engine department.

'Then to the 412T1,' he reflects with a sigh. 'There again, we started to fall foul of the politics. The fundamental thing which cocked it all up was the cooling, because the engine department, under Mr Lombardi, did not do what I asked them to do, which was to balance the water flows, side to side. We had an asymmetric cooling system; the oil on one side, which in those days on the V12 was a pretty big radiator, and the water was then a small radiator on that side and a larger one on the other.

'We'd built some full-sized mock-ups and went to MIRA (the Motor Industry Research Association) to test full-size radiator heat output using hot water in the radiators. We'd gone the whole hog. Put it in a wind tunnel, measured the heat output, really went to town, the idea being that we reduce the drag in the radiator system because the heat output from the V12 was high.

'So I put extra big radiators in it, paid the price with a bit of extra weight, but the idea was we would flow the air through it very slowly which meant that

In 1993, Ferrari had a difficult season with this type F93A which was essentially a reworked version of the previous year's machine (Allsport).

the pressure drop losses were small, re-energising the air flow out of the end of the pod which was at the same pressure as going into the pod. So the system drag would be zero.

'We reckoned we were very close to zero drag and I also tried to minimise the side pod drag. We then started running the car and we had real problems. When we should have been running blanking, we were having to open extra apertures on the side pod. We struggled. My initial reaction was hell, what have we done wrong? Having said all that, the first part of the season wasn't that bad. Second on the grid at Canada and third in the race.

'For the honour of Italy'

The early 1970s were dark days at Maranello. The superb, high-revving 3-litre flat-12 was progressively developed into a formidably competitive engine, but Ferrari's chassis technology simply couldn't keep pace. The team's idea of monocoque construction – de rigueur in F1 since the advent of Colin Chapman's Lotus 25 almost a decade earlier – was a base of small-diameter tubing panelled in aluminium sheeting.

Put simply, Enzo Ferrari had always done things His Way. Ever since his small company had matured into an F1 force to be reckoned with, he radiated an unquestioning faith that his team knew how best to tackle any technical challenge.

He could also be extraordinarily ungracious. By the summer of 1955, the rival Lancia F1 team was overwhelmed by financial problems and its delicious Vittorio Jano-designed D50s seemed destined for the scrapheap. These products of the famous Turin-based manufacturer were, by common consensus, true state-of-the-art Grand Prix machines, easily of a calibre matching the contemporary rival Mercedes-Benz W196s.

Amazingly, Fiat then stumped up around £30,000 a year for Ferrari to take over the D50 project and continue what was emotionally characterised as an F1 fight 'for the honour of Italy against the overwhelming might of the Germans'.

The reality of this situation was that Ferrari had been handed a ready-made competitive lifeline. His own type 555 'Super Squalos' had been struggling to produce competitive performances in the early races of 1955 and now circumstances had presented him, gratis, with the best Grand Prix chassis/engine combination in the business. All he had to do was a nifty touch of badge engineering.

Yet there were signs that he resented Fiat's largesse, an attitude which would come to seem ironic slightly more than a decade later when the Italian motor giant rescued Enzo's own near-bankrupt company from commercial oblivion. Over the next two seasons, the Lancia D50s were progressively bastardised into Maranello specials and, in their final incarnation as the 1957 Ferrari 801, failed to win a single World Championship Grand Prix.

'But Mike Coughlan (Barnard's right-hand man at FDD) and I were literally rushing carbon components to the airport, literally still hot. Got off the plane, went to see Nigel Stepney (the team's chief mechanic), worked all night and got them fitted. But the real problem was that the water system was out of balance – two-thirds of the water flow went through the small radiator, one third through the big radiator. That was because the pressure drops hadn't been balanced on the engine. Then turning vanes – barge boards – arrived on the scene, and with our sidepods it was difficult to fit them.

'So I let them put on the short side pods, but at the same time we made new radiators to go with them, but somebody must have looked at the system because, low and behold, a by-pass tube appeared going from one radiator to another. They'd put the radiators on the dyno with the engine and seen the problem. Of course, that was the answer. If we had balanced the system earlier, we would never have touched the sidepod from a cooling point of view.'

There were also deeper considerations to be confronted as far as engines were concerned. Ferrari seemed deeply, emotionally and symbolically wedded to the V12 cylinder configuration. That had seemed fine when Barnard outlined the type 640 design in early 1988, but by 1992 Renault and Honda had proved that the V10 route was the way to go. Persuading Maranello that this configuration offered the best

Previous pages: Gerhard ready for business in the cockpit of the Ferrari 412T2, viewing the instruments clearly thanks to the distinctive cutaway steering wheel design (LAT).

compromise between weight, fuel consumption, power and ease of overall packaging proved to be something else again.

When he came back on board, Barnard ruffled a few traditionalist feathers by announcing that, in his view, the V12 cylinder configuration was now played out. Ferrari needed another engine, either a V10 or even a V8.

Some months later, Barnard was chatting to Stuart Grove, a member of the Cosworth F1 engine design team who came highly recommended by some of the key personnel at the famous Northampton engine specialist. Grove had previously been deeply involved in the HB V8 engine design used to such promising effect by Benetton. Barnard took him on and he was duly installed at Maranello to investigate and outline a new Ferrari F1 engine specification.

Grove worked away and duly completed a 3.5-litre V8 design for the Italian team. No metal was ever cut, however. Maranello's in-built defence mechanism – its dark suspicion of outsiders – somehow conspired to isolate Grove and his small team of engineers. After more than a year's work, he reported to Barnard that he felt frustrated. In his estimation, nobody was really interested in the V8. The highly regarded Grove left and went to Ilmor. 'He was a very good guy,' says Barnard. 'I had a lot of respect for him and he brought some fresh thinking to the business.'

Then there was the question of a V10. In an effort to get such an engine configuration quickly, they discussed a possible collaboration with ace engine builder Brian Hart. Claudio Lombardi flew over from Italy and accompanied Barnard to Hart's compact premises in Harlow, Essex, where they watched Brian's V10 running on the test bed one evening. There were all sorts of proposals; possibly badging Hart's engine as a Ferrari for a short-term fix, employing Brian as a consultant.

Who knows the secrets behind these gates? Ferrari's racing headquarters on Maranello's evocatively titled Via Alberto Ascari (Ferrari UK).

Gerhard Berger confers with John Barnard. Driver and designer developed a healthy professional respect, Barnard clearly feeling that the Austrian was generally more logical and analytical than Alesi (LAT).

'I was pushing any way I could to get things moving on the engine side,' recalls Barnard with an air of frustration. But not until the new 3-litre V10 for 1996 did he have his way and the V12 get consigned to the history books.

Barnard's 1995 design was a high-nose challenger on which the front lower suspension pick-up points were mounted outside the lower edge of the monocoque itself. He had also experimented with the means of attaching the upper wishbones to the outer chassis wall. He used both uni-ball joints and flexures (suspension joints) in which the only flexibility was the material of the joint itself. The flexures were intended to confer additional ride stiffness on the car as well as reducing operating friction.

The side pods began to flare outwards from the monocoque at the point where the under-car aerodynamic 'splitter' began. Suspension was by means of double wishbones and pushrods with the coil spring/dampers at the front and torsion bars at the rear, for packaging reasons. At the rear, with characteristic attention to detail, Barnard incorporated an incredibly complex-looking diffuser panel beneath which were included six vertical vanes designed to control the lateral pressure gradient beneath the end of the car.

As far as engines were concerned, the 412T1 started the year equipped with an up-rated version of the previous season's 65-degree type 041 V12 which developed around 775bhp at 15,300rpm. This seven bearing unit had proved consistently frail when revved to over the 15,000rpm mark. However, Claudio Lombardi's engine department was also working on a new 75-degree V12, tipped to develop 820bhp at 15,800rpm, and that would gradually be phased in later in the year. The transmission was by means of a transverse six-speed gearbox within a chrome-molybdenum casing which helped to provide a stiffer, more rigid overall chassis structure.

Reflecting on the 412T2, with its low nose and classical good looks, Barnard acknowledges that the current F1 aerodynamic options are finely balanced. So what were the pros and cons of the 1994 412T1 (high nose) and the 1995 412T2 (low nose)?

'You can make a case either way,' says Barnard. 'Looking back on it, in 1995 we didn't have the most efficient aerodynamic car. We had a very driveable car, but ultimately we didn't have as absolutely effective an aerodynamic package as the Williams FW17.

'Mid-season the development went to Maranello and we were struggling a bit with the numbers from the wind tunnel not really stacking up with what was happening on the track, so that was another problem. It seems to me that you can choose a high nose or low nose, and develop those with the front wing system and the rest of the car, to end up in a largely similar condition.

'We probably should have undercut the 412T2 monocoque to get the absolute maximum out of it. But the bottom line is that any design is interactive; what you do at the front affects what works well at the back. You can do little tiny tweaks which will completely change the air flow along the bottom of the car, to the point where you could look at two cars and hardly see the difference. But one would work and one wouldn't.

'I would class the nose position on the 1996 car as intermediate.' If it works sufficiently well then Maranello may well carry on with the development while Barnard's team looks at the car in a different direction, from the nose back, 'to see if we can evaluate an alternative concept'.

Taken as a whole, the Ferrari Design & Development set-up works well. It is responsible for initiating and finalising the entire F1 car design concepts, Barnard sometimes preferring to outline the initial concept of the car on a traditional drawing board before his colleagues get down to the nitty gritty detail on CAD/CAM design stations which are linked to the Maranello factory.

The UK-based operation also manufactures various suspension and carbon-fibre chassis components, as well as carrying out static rig testing on items such as pushrod assemblies and torsion bars. However, the complete car build takes place at Maranello and once Barnard's design group has signed off the final concept, the operation of the new cars is effectively assumed by the racing arm of the company, leaving Ferrari Design & Development to press ahead with long-term research work for future machines.

Chapter Four

The men at the wheel

Gerhard Berger is a tall, bounding extrovert Austrian whose two stints at Ferrari, from 1987 to 1989 and 1993 to 1995, endeared him to the team as one of the most popular and easy-going of personalities.

His Grand Prix debut had come at the wheel of an ATS-BMW in 1984 and he drove for Arrows and Benetton before joining Ferrari. He had arrived at Maranello on the strength of his fine 1986 season at the wheel of a Benetton-BMW, during which he scored a tactically lucky win in the Mexican Grand Prix. More importantly, he ended a two and a half year dearth of Ferrari victories when he won the 1987 Japanese race at Suzuka.

Mid-way through 1989 Berger began to think that the stress of trying to compete with Nigel Mansell as a team-mate was becoming a little too much. Surely, he reasoned, if you want to really test yourself against a team-mate, McLaren was the place to go? As a result, he signed on the dotted line to partner Ayrton Senna in the Honda-powered line-up. The Austrian entered his first McLaren season motivated by enormous self-belief, only to find that Senna was on a level above mere mortals when it came to handling a Grand Prix car.

It says much for Gerhard's strength of character and ability to come to terms with reality that he quickly became integrated into the McLaren line-up.

Once he had mentally accepted the fact that he was not in the same class as the brilliant Brazilian, Berger knuckled down to forge a close and cordial relationship with him. In short, Ayrton taught him a great deal about professionalism, application and commitment, while Berger's influence helped Senna to lighten up away from the cockpit and learn to shelve his intensity and have fun. Many's the tale told in pit and paddock of Berger's practical jokes on hapless colleagues – and of Senna's imaginative reprisals.

For all his foibles, Senna was a deeply sensitive man who made friends only after they had proved themselves to him. People tended to be overly-deferential to him, but Gerhard was always honest and candid, even when it hurt. Senna came to appreciate that. He felt he could rely on Gerhard absolutely and the Austrian became one of his few genuinely close friends in the motor racing milieu.

Gerhard Berger's easy-going nature concealed a measured professionalism however, even though there were those within the F1 business who doubted whether he was sufficiently committed to be a serious contender. The reality was that he always applied a rational and balanced attitude to his motor racing. He was a great team player and, for all his off-track light-heartedness, grew in stature over the years to the point where even the sport's governing body came to regard him as one of the most mature, logical representatives of the F1 drivers' lobby.

Gerhard Berger...his easy-going nature concealed a measured professionalism (LAT).

Berger's return to Ferrari in 1993 came as a surprise to many observers. He had fitted very well into the McLaren organisation and was much liked by team chief Ron Dennis. Yet all this geniality could not conceal the fact that he was still working in Ayrton's shadow. It was an experience which had made Gerhard a better, more rounded performer, but now it was time to strike out again and see what he could make of his career in his own right.

There were other considerations, of course. McLaren was offering only a $3 million retainer; Luca di Montezemolo proposed $10 million. Gerhard, a man with a cute eye for a deal, was swayed by the attractions of returning to Maranello. Yet it was a measure of his standing at McLaren that Dennis remarked: 'I have told Gerhard, for him the McLaren door will always be open'.

The cheerful Austrian was also a good negotiator, swapping back to Ferrari with a number one contract. Yet 1993 was a bad year for Gerhard. His Ferrari return was punctuated by far too many off-track excursions and seemingly inexplicable collisions for a driver of his undoubted calibre. There must have been times when Montezemolo wondered what on earth he had been paying for. Nevertheless, if one could look past his efforts in shovelling Hill off the road at Monaco, his slowing-down lap collision with Alesi during qualifying at Monza, and his absurd Spa crash into Blundell's Ligier, Berger left some decent results on the record book. Sixth in South Africa, Spain, and Germany, fifth in Australia, fourth in Canada, and third in Hungary went some way towards restoring his rather shaky image.

Berger had come back into the team as number one. It was a decision which Alesi found hard to deal with and it was well into 1994 before he was really happy with the relationship.

'Gerhard and Alain were very different people,' mused Jean in the summer of 1994. 'Alain was the same nationality as me, and a three-times World Champion. He was an example for me to follow and I tried to do exactly that because I wanted to be like him.

'However, with Gerhard alongside me in the team, it has been more of a fight, because when he came back to Ferrari in 1993, he had a very strong contract, a first driver contract, so I was not so happy. But I proved to the team that I was able to be very quick too, so – because Gerhard is a very sympathetic person – we adjusted the contract for 1994 and now there is no specific number one.

'I did find the situation very difficult and hard to accept. But now it is very good because Gerhard is not only very quick, but he is a non-political person. At Ferrari it is very important to have a driver like that.' In reality, Gerhard accepted the effective demotion to 'joint number one' status out of pragmatic good grace. It was just too emotionally tiring to have the volatile Alesi always grumbling about the situation, so he gave way.

Yet behind that free-wheeling facade, Berger's astute touch has not deserted him. In 1995, weighing up the options, he rightly concluded that Michael Schumacher would be maximum aggravation as a Maranello team-mate for the following season. With his career perhaps now peaking out, he shrewdly switched to Benetton and left the field open for Eddie Irvine to deal with the challenge of keeping pace with das Wunderkind.

The race morning warm-up for the 1986 United States GP at Detroit. Nigel Mansell goes past at the wheel of a Ferrari. I beg your pardon? The previous night's alcoholic revelry must have gone on a bottle or two beyond what was intended. Yesterday he was in a Williams-Honda.

There was no reason to panic. Sure enough, it was Nigel Mansell's helmet – his spare helmet, actually – on short-term loan to Stefan Johansson, the Swedish Ferrari driver

Nigel Mansell...frustrated and dismayed after a succession of mechanical failures (LAT).

having somehow mislaid his own bone dome. It would be another three years before Nigel would finally make Maranello his spiritual, albeit temporary, motor racing home. Mansell still claims the record as Britain's statistically most successful F1 driver with a total of 31 Grand Prix victories to his credit, ranking third in the all-time winners' stakes after Prost and Senna (with 51 and 41 wins respectively). Yet only three of those triumphs were achieved at Ferrari, a team he joined after a dismal 1988 season at Williams struggling with an uncompetitive Judd V8 engine.

Originally promoted to F1 by Lotus founder Colin Chapman, Mansell did not make his talent immediately evident. In those early days the moustachioed driver from Birmingham seemed strong on self-opinionated over-confidence and weak on results. Yet his detractors were soon in for a surprise. Signed by Frank Williams as a steady number two for Keke Rosberg in 1985, Mansell emerged as an assured performer with lightning reflexes and heroic car control.

But by the summer of 1988, he had tired of Williams. The team was no longer able to provide him with competitive machinery and the romantic notion of riding to the rescue of Ferrari's fortunes was too much for the Englishman to resist. With his bank account buttressed by a reassuring multi-million dollar retainer, he signed for the Prancing Horse and sealed the deal with a dream-like maiden victory in the 1989 Brazilian GP at Rio.

That same season also saw him score a brilliantly opportunistic victory in the Hungarian GP, jumping ahead of Ayrton Senna's McLaren-Honda after the Brazilian found himself momentarily boxed in as he came up to lap a slower car. It was a win which represented the height of Mansell's achievement at the wheel of one of the Italian cars.

In 1990 Mansell found himself tactically outmanoeuvred at Ferrari by newcomer Alain Prost. Frustrated and dismayed after a succession of mechanical failures, on the evening after he failed to finish the British GP at Silverstone Nigel announced that he would retire from F1 at the end of the season. As things transpired, he eventually changed his mind, signed for Williams in 1991 and finally nailed down that elusive World Championship the following year.

Long after his departure from Maranello, Mansell continued to maintain his links with Ferrari with a dealership – Nigel Mansell Sports Cars – near Blandford in Dorset. During his time as a Ferrari driver his private jet also carried a Prancing Horse logo on its fuselage. It seemed an unusually sentimental touch from a driver widely regarded as one of the hardest-nosed operators in the F1 business.

Monza, 1989. The Italian Grand Prix had just finished and Alain Prost is being fêted as a hero for his victory by the delighted *tifosi*. Not that Prost had won the race in a Ferrari, mind you. He was at the wheel of a red and white McLaren-Honda. But the news was already announced that the brilliant Frenchman had signed a contract for 1990 to drive for the Prancing Horse. The delight projected by the seething, joyful crowd said it all: Ferrari's future was looking good.

Then Alain did something quite out of character. In an emotional gesture to cement his forthcoming bond with the Italian fans, he leaned over the balcony and dropped the winner's trophy into the maelstrom of frenzied humanity below. At a symbolic stroke, one sensed he had written *finis* to his relationship with McLaren. For the moment, at least.

Ron Dennis, the McLaren team chief, was reduced to simmering silence, such was his anger. It was his view that Alain, in a cheap bid for popularity, breached the protocol which dictated that McLaren trophies belonged to the team. Yet his annoyance was tempered by a sense of disappointment. Now he knew that one of the most precious driver/entrant relationships of all time had run its course.

Alain Prost...warned Ferrari that to be competitive they would have to speed up their technical development (LAT).

When Prost went to Ferrari in 1990, he was reigning World Champion with two previous titles with McLaren already to his credit. He had shaped a matchless CV in the junior formulae and had developed a reputation as a development driver and tester. A compact Charles Aznavour lookalike, he was popular, gregarious – and blessed with a personality to melt female hearts.

Prost did a fine job for Ferrari in his first season. He had the proven stature and gravitas which, perhaps, Nigel Mansell lacked as a consequence of not having yet won a World Championship. Come the day Alain, with his five wins and two second places, got closer to winning Maranello a title than anybody since Jody Scheckter in 1979. Then came Senna's intervention at Suzuka and the party was over for that season.

In 1991, Ferrari simply refused to hear Prost's warnings that to be competitive they would have to speed up the pace of technical development. Alain became downcast and preoccupied with a situation he could not control.

It was all horribly familiar. Back in 1983, Prost had warned Renault to raise their game if they didn't want to lose the championship to Nelson Piquet's Brabham-BMW. The French car company did just that. Then they made Prost the fall guy and fired him. In 1991, one race from the end of the season, Ferrari effectively did just the same. Prost was out.

Alesi had originally sprung to prominence in 1987 when he won the French F3 Championship, his path to F1 subsequently smoothed by winning the 1989 European F3000 Championship driving for the Silverstone-based Jordan team. Eight F1 grands prix guest driving for Tyrrell that year, followed by a move to Tyrrell proper in 1990, and his future looked rosy. Eddie Jordan subsequently received a multi-million dollar boost to his fortunes from the commission he received in brokering Alesi's Ferrari contract.

When Jean Alesi joined Ferrari at the start of the 1991 season, as partner to Alain Prost, he brought with him an enormous sense of enthusiasm, motivation and expectancy. After all, here was the young French-Sicilian who had diced so cheekily with Ayrton Senna's McLaren-Honda at Phoenix only 12 months earlier, finishing a strong second to the peerless Brazilian. He also finished a brilliant second to Senna three races later at Monaco, matching Ayrton's own achievement six years earlier.

Surely, this daredevil, old-style racer – who only knew one way to compete, flat out – would be the driver with the talent to consolidate the achievements which had taken Prost so close to the 1990 World Championship. Frustratingly not. Five seasons later, he would be dropped by Ferrari having only scored a single win, in the 1995 Canadian GP.

'I expected a lot,' reflected Alesi on the subject of his first season at Ferrari. 'I joined Maranello believing that I could win from the start, but after a few races I realised that the car was not sufficiently competitive against the McLaren-Hondas and that the team was not working together well. To be honest, it was a mess.

'People have criticised me for staying at Ferrari against all logic, for wasting my youth and my image. But I knew one day I would get there.' Nevertheless, by the time Jean shuffled out of the Maranello equation at the end of 1995, it was clear that his image had suffered long-term damage. He had come to be regarded as F1's 'Nearly Man'. He had the capability in terms of sheer speed and lightning reflexes, but his ability to draw together all those disparate qualities into a cohesive, winning package was seriously doubted.

Jean Alesi...a brilliant or a wild performer depending on his mood at that particular instant (Allsport).

Gianni Morbidelli...one of the most under-rated of F1 talents (LAT).

It was a far cry from the optimistic note on which he had joined Maranello. But the period as Prost's team-mate was immensely valuable to Jean, who has always been quick to credit the gifted Frenchman.

'I was able to learn my job with a big team alongside a masterful driver,' he explained. 'Alain Prost is the only driver for whom I feel absolute veneration; both for the man and the driver. Before I started in Formula 1, he was my hero. But once I got into the system, I found him cold, distant and impossible to get close to. I didn't like him and he wasn't happy about my arrival at Ferrari.

'He was afraid that two French drivers at Ferrari would produce a lot of controversy and destroy all his work; but I did not try to be a big driver. I put myself at his service like a true team-mate. I got to know him, he learned to appreciate me and, together, we fought the mountains of problems we encountered. When Alain left the Scuderia suddenly, I was a bit lost.

'Things got bad after that. I paid a high price, dearer than a lot of drivers because I really take my job seriously. Then I could see it was getting better and I was able to forget everything in the past once I scored that first victory at Montreal.'

When the triple World Champion was fired at the end of 1991, Alesi had to assume the mantle of team leader for 1992. This proved to be less than successful. In the histrionic atmosphere of Maranello – steeped in history and mystique, riven with Latin intrigue – his own emotions frequently got the better of him and his mood was in no way improved when Gerhard Berger was signed as *de facto* number one in the 1993 Ferrari line-up. Berger would subsequently informally agree to have his contract amended to accommodate Jean on an equal standing. It made life in the pit lane less stressful.

Yet by the start of the 1994 season, Alesi was being run ragged by the strain of failing to break his Grand Prix duck. He should have won commandingly at Monza, so his somewhat fortuitous victory at Montreal in the summer of 1995 was rightly regarded as having at last balanced the results books.

Alesi's volatile nature was not best suited to Maranello. His hair-trigger temperament, combined with a tendency to shoot from the hip when it came to aiming criticism at the management, was all too much. Luca di Montezemolo had little choice but to place the hemlock in front of him when it became clear that Michael Schumacher was willing to join Ferrari for 1996.

It only remained to be seen whether Benetton would provide a more calming environment in which Alesi would flourish as an ex-Ferrari driver.

Gianni Morbidelli was the youngest F1 driver of all during the 1991 season, having signed a Ferrari testing contract at the age of 21 and made his F1 debut for the Dallara team shortly after his 22nd birthday. Gianni came from a motorsport background, his father manufacturing Morbidelli racing bikes which contested the 125cc and 350cc international classes during the early 1970s.

In 1991 Gianni was signed to drive for the Minardi team, then using Ferrari V12 engines, and switched to Maranello's works team as Alain Prost's successor for that season's finale in Australia only days after the Frenchman was fired. Morbidelli drove well to finish sixth. He has since been regarded as one of the most underrated of F1 talents, well worth a regular place with a top team.

When Ivan Capelli took his March-Judd to a close second place behind Alain Prost's McLaren in the 1988 Portuguese GP many felt that this pleasantly open 25-year old from Milan stood poised to claim the mantle as Italy's most promising F1 talent.

Yet perhaps Capelli was just too self-effacing for the ruthless cut and thrust of top-line motor racing politics. At Estoril, and again in 1990 when, in a Leyton House-Judd, he finished second to Alain in the French GP, he talked deferentially about how proud he had been to stand up there on the rostrum 'alongside Mr Prost'. He eventually received his reward with promotion to the Ferrari F1 team partnering Alesi in 1992, but, sadly, he had drawn the wrong season for such high-profile attention and was worn down by the disappointment.

A great animal lover, Capelli seemed too sensitive and gentle a man in the literal sense of the word. When some mindlessly cruel buffoon mowed down a flock of ducks on the approach road to the paddock at Montreal during the Canadian GP weekend, Ivan was utterly distraught. To him, their plight was of far more consequence than anything which might have taken place out on the race track.

Ivan Capelli...didn't have the aggressive edge to deal with the Ferrari situation (LAT).

Michael Schumacher arrived at Ferrari in 1996 with impeccable credentials, the logical successor to the late Ayrton Senna as F1's most dynamic performer. Double World Champion for Benetton in 1994 and 1995, he was the quickest, most mature and comprehensively rounded talent of all. No matter that he projected a certain Germanic arrogance to those who could not get close enough to know him.

The German star's F1 achievements are too recent, too frequently quoted and too much an essential element of this volume to need recounting in detail here. Suffice to

Michael Schumacher...bringing a logical, North European mindset to the Maranello machinations (LAT).

say that one of the most telling snapshots of his true character was seen at the 1996 Brazilian GP when his wife Corinna adopted a rather mangy stray dog which they found wandering around the paddock on their arrival at Interlagos.

Over the next couple of days, while concentrating on the F1 business of the weekend, Michael and his wife found time to arrange for the animal to be treated by a local vet and organised its transport back to Germany to begin a new life as a member of the Schumacher household.

Eddie Irvine will always be remembered in the F1 history book as the cheeky newcomer who came within inches of a punch from Ayrton Senna after the Brazilian driver reckoned he'd unnecessarily held up his McLaren during the 1993 Japanese GP.

It was absolutely characteristic of Irvine – imbued with the same sense of relaxed irreverence which so distinguished James Hunt's career – that he wasn't in the least bit intimidated by his august senior colleague.

The Ulsterman was given his F1 break by Eddie Jordan but spent only two years driving for his former F3000 entrant before deciding that his own F1 talent was growing faster than that of his employer.

First targeted by Ferrari as a possible candidate as early as May 1995, Irvine was deemed by the paddock pundits to be a suitable team-mate for Schumacher having both a strong personality and the wit to publicly accept being the second driver. His sister Sonia, a qualified physiotherapist, also joined the team to make the Maranello line-up something of a family affair as well as keeping her younger brother in line. And so it proved.

At the first race of the season in Melbourne, Eddie was signing a batch of autographs when Sonia slipped in a birthday card for their father. Irvine signed it without thinking, only to be brought up sharp when his sister remarked 'Eddie, I think Dad knows what your surname is!'

Eddie Irvine...never intimidated by august senior colleagues (LAT).

Chapter Five

Moments in the sun

Any consideration of Gerhard Berger's contribution to Ferrari's renaissance must be analysed against the events, triumphs and disasters of the 1994 season. By then Barnard was well into the swing of his three-year development programme at FDD and decided to have a totally fresh look at the possible design parameters defined by the current F1 technical regulations.

He discussed the prospects for the forthcoming season in some detail with both Montezemolo and Fiat boss Gianni Agnelli, advising them that the new car – the 412T1 – could reasonably be expected to come on strongly in the second half of the year. This would logically lead to a car which might be a regular winner in 1995, so that a tilt at the World Championship might be expected in 1996.

The 1994 season started with Alesi taking a strong third place behind Michael Schumacher's Benetton and Damon Hill's Williams in the Brazilian GP, but Jean then damaged his back in a testing accident at Mugello and had to sit out the next two rounds of the championship. His place for the Pacific GP at Japan's new Aida circuit and the San Marino GP at Imola was taken by test driver Nicola Larini.

Of course, this was the first season in which the F1 technical regulations stipulated a ban on any sort of electronic driver aids. Thus, when the FIA's technical delegate Charlie Whiting was alerted to a possible irregularity after detecting a fluttering engine note on Larini's car during the first free practice session at Aida, Ferrari seemed to have been catapulted straight into the centre of the first controversy of a bruising season.

It appeared that Ferrari was using a variable rev limiter and, after consultation with Sporting Director Jean Todt, Whiting advised Ferrari not to use it again for the balance of the weekend while the question of its possible illegality was examined. Several rival teams were sceptical, but Ferrari was cleared of breaching the rules.

A week later, the FIA issued a communique on the matter. 'In essence, these devices change the characteristics of the engine according to certain predetermined instructions,' read the text. 'The "map" of the engine, or the permissible throttle opening, or the rev limit, may be different in each gear. Alternatively, the characteristics of the engine may be changed according to the whereabouts of the car on the circuit, or be set at will by the driver. Devices of this kind are not traction control because they are not influenced in any way by the behaviour of the rear wheels.' It was unsurprising that some rivals didn't see it that way, many contending that Ferrari's actions had effectively amounted to a breach of the regulations because they had interfered with the amount of power given by the engine at a given speed by means of overriding the driver's throttle input.

'The question that remains is what was Ferrari using this system for,' said Patrick

1994 was a year Gerhard Berger would never forget (LAT).

Ferrari test driver Nicola Larini deputised for the injured Jean Alesi at Aida, but found himself spearing through the gravel trap into Ayrton Senna's Williams-Renault after the Brazilian was edged into a spin by Mika Hakkinen's McLaren (LAT).

Head, Williams Technical Director. 'Traction control is not defined specifically in the regulations, so it is my opinion that any means of pre-setting power levels in this way is intended to have a similar effect.'

At the start of the Pacific GP, Larini ploughed into the gravel trap at the first corner, but Berger survived to finish second behind Michael Schumacher's Benetton. Ferrari was now second in the Constructors' Championship with two of the season's 16 races completed.

The next race on the schedule was the ill-fated San Marino GP where Ferrari used the new 75-degree engine to qualify third behind Senna and Schumacher, proving that the latest V12 had the power to compete with both Renault V10 and Ford V8. However, by the time Gerhard took up his position on the starting grid, he had been shaken to the very core of his soul by the death of fellow Austrian Roland Ratzenberger whose Simtek had crashed in second qualifying on the 180mph approach to the Tosa left-hander.

Gerhard would have been less than human had his mind not flashed back to his fiery accident at the same circuit five years before. 'When I saw the accident on television, I found myself shaking in the car,' he later confessed. 'But, of course, in our job we must

Previous pages: Alesi is wheel-to-wheel with team-mate Gerhard Berger as they chase Michael Schumacher's winning Benetton B194 round the opening lap of the Canadian GP at Montreal, eventually finishing third and fourth (ICN UK Bureau).

sometimes be prepared to see these things. Then I got out of the car and went into the motorhome, still shaking. But the question for me was not whether I was going to drive today, but whether I was going to drive tomorrow, or at any time in the future.'

The tragedy – first death at a GP meeting for 12 years – would be multiplied a hundredfold on race day when Ayrton Senna crashed fatally at Tamburello whilst leading the opening stages of the race. The Brazilian's Williams had slammed into the wall, then bounced back onto the edge of the circuit, scattering mechanical debris in all directions. The race was immediately red-flagged to a halt – not a second too soon for Gerhard whose Ferrari had run over part of the Williams nose section as it passed the accident scene.

When Gerhard climbed out and examined the damage to his own car, he found that the front suspension on the right-hand side was only hanging on by a sliver of metal. It was a discovery which did little to sharpen his appetite for any further racing. Yet, come the re-start, Gerhard threw himself into the fray with single-minded commitment, almost as if by totally immersing himself in the business of the afternoon he could

Alesi lands in the gravel trap at Magny-Cours during the 1994 French GP after spinning off, then collecting the hapless Rubens Barrichello's Jordan as he attempted to regain the circuit (ICN UK Bureau).

somehow take his mind off his fears about Senna's condition.

For 11 laps, he stormed round wheel-to-wheel with Schumacher's Benetton, then pulled into the pits. Drained of emotion and commitment, he was further undermined by what he felt was a worrying rear-end handling imbalance from his car. Jean Todt put a sympathetic hand on his shoulder and told him he'd done more than enough. Gerhard climbed from the car and walked away into the garage, leaving Larini to come home second behind Schumacher.

Later that evening, Gerhard travelled to the Maggiore hospital at Bologna. His dear friend Ayrton was now in a deep coma, all brain activity having ceased. Berger was with Senna shortly before he was officially pronounced dead and formally identified him on behalf of the Senna family. Then he left for Austria. Others could not make a start at guessing what turbulent thoughts were going through the mind of this fine man.

The following Thursday, Gerhard led the pallbearers at Senna's funeral in Sao Paulo's Morumbi cemetery. He then climbed aboard an overnight flight to Paris, picked up his private jet and flew to Austria for Roland Ratzenberger's funeral. Drained beyond

...The long walk back (LAT).

Mutual delight as Alesi wins second place at Silverstone (LAT).

measure, he was no longer certain whether he wanted any part in the Formula 1 business.

'I am in a situation at the moment in which I have absolutely no desire to get into a racing car,' he said in the run-up to the Monaco Grand Prix, just a fortnight after Imola. 'We were supposed to have tested this week to prepare for Monaco, but I just didn't want to do it because I don't think I'm ready for it yet.

'I have always raced with my heart. I lived for it. Racing is what I've done for my whole life. However, if my feelings tell me that I am unable to take the risks required, then I will quit. My big problem at the moment is that I have lost faith in (F1) technology. I have had so many accidents in which technical failure was the cause that I have lost confidence.'

Berger eventually reversed his decision, although his confidence was again shaken by the serious accident which befell another compatriot, the Sauber driver Karl Wendlinger, during practice at Monaco. The days of pain seemed without end, but Berger kept racing. Moreover, at Monaco he finished a storming third behind Schumacher and Martin Brundle's McLaren-Peugeot, the only other competitor to complete the full 78-lap distance.

'That first morning in the car at Monte Carlo was very important, you know,' he told *Autosport*'s Nigel Roebuck later in the summer of 1994. 'I knew I wanted to go on racing, but perhaps there would be something inside now that said "be careful". But I

Before the start of the 1994 German GP at Hockenheim, Berger and Alesi pose for the cameras. A moment of high tension and enormous expectancy (LAT).

was immediately quick and, within two laps, knew that everything would be all right.

'That was just as well, because I wasn't prepared for what would happen if I didn't feel that way. Then I would have faced a real problem. Racing is my life.'

One effect of the Imola tragedy was to revitalise the role of the Grand Prix Drivers' Association and Gerhard would take an important part in steadying this particular helm. Many of the younger drivers were distraught and confused, having never previously experienced tragedy on anything approaching this scale. Berger did a good job behind the scenes to soothe their concerns.

At Monaco the FIA also introduced a dramatic list of changes to the F1 technical regulations to slow the cars, as a direct result of the Imola weekend. These included such drastic revisions to the aerodynamic configuration of the cars that John Barnard

Watched over by his own hugely enlarged image, Gerhard Berger is pushed out of the pit garage (Allsport).

was moved to remark that it looked as though FIA President Max Mosley had reversed his view that a knee-jerk reaction to the disastrous weekend in Italy was the last thing the sport really needed.

'We're being presented with a *fait accompli*,' noted Barnard. 'I doubt the measures would have been announced now were it not for Wendlinger's accident.' Yet the FIA had to do something and, more importantly, be seen to do something in the eyes of governments and sporting authorities across the world. Make no mistake, Formula 1 safety was under the global microscope.

Meanwhile, the development of the 412T1 continued apace. The new car's initial tendency towards slow speed understeer was gradually ironed out. Unfortunately, Barnard's original design concept was significantly changed in response to the rule

Previous pages: Berger leads Alesi away from the Hockenheim grid as the tailenders become embroiled in their own private accident (LAT). Above: Ahead of the crowd (LAT).

changes and for the French GP a heavily revised aerodynamic package was evolved, including the unsightly turning vanes ahead of the side pod entry on either side of what would now become known as the 412T1B.

The need to shorten the front wing end plates, as well as raising the wing itself, in response to the new regulations, had obliged Ferrari to run increased nose wing flap angles in an effort to claw back some of the front-end downforce. This reduced the air flow to the water radiators which, as explained earlier, had already shown signs of being marginal on cooling.

Another rule change imposed by the FIA called for venting of the engine airboxes, thereby reducing the pressure build-up in the induction system and, in theory, contributing towards a reduction in power. Pump fuel was also required, but Ferrari was again at the centre of attention during qualifying for the Canadian GP where the team was asked by the FIA Technical Delegate to add an additional rearward vent on

At last! Gerhard Berger ends the longest drought in Ferrari F1 history with a storming victory in the 1994 German GP (LAT).

their airboxes in the aftermath of complaints from some rival teams.

Alesi, who had been quickest on the first day, dropped to second behind Schumacher's Benetton in the final grid order. Some people regarded this as evidence that his Ferrari had benefited from that airbox 'advantage' in the first session, but Jean Todt vigorously rebutted such suggestions.

'As to the rumours flying around some of the English teams who seem to have a grudge against us, I cannot accept their comments,' he said trenchantly. 'Ferrari are complying with the regulations here in Montreal, as they always have done and always will do. To say that our air intake, which was seen and approved by the FIA on Thursday, does not comply with the regulations, or that we are using special fuel, is only the reaction of people who refuse to believe that we are competitive again. As a gesture of goodwill, and under no obligation, we put another hole in the airbox of the 412T1 and, as all could see, this made no difference.'

Alesi and Berger lined up second and third, finishing third and fourth in the race. It was a good result which consolidated Ferrari's second place in the Constructors' Championship, albeit 25 points behind Benetton. The French GP at Magny-Cours continued in much the same vein with Berger third – Alesi dropped out after a stupid collision with the Jordan 194 of Rubens Barrichello.

The British GP at Silverstone saw both Ferrari drivers benefiting from the use of the new 75-degree V12 engines during qualifying, Gerhard qualifying third only two-hundredths of a second away from Hill's pole position in the Williams. In fact, Berger might well have qualified fastest of all had he not slid into the

Start of the Belgian GP with Alesi's Ferrari wheel-locking its way up the inside of Eddie Irvine's Jordan as Schumacher takes the lead from pole man Rubens Barrichello (ICN UK Bureau).

retaining wall on the exit of the pit lane as he accelerated out for his final run with only seven minutes of the Saturday session left to go. It was an inexplicable lapse, which he confessed was nobody's fault but his own. Gerhard tried to limp back to the pits, but the left front wheel rim was broken and he eventually spun to a gentle halt out on the circuit.

Come the race, Berger opted for a single refuelling stop, Hill and Schumacher deciding on two. This allowed Gerhard to lead from lap 18 to 21, but he dropped out 11 laps later because of engine failure. Alesi finished second, but with Hill winning strongly, Williams now moved ahead of Ferrari to hold second place in the Constructors' Championship table.

Hockenheim turned out to be a truly historic weekend for Maranello. It began on a rather dismal note when Berger's older 65-degree V12 exploded spectacularly on Friday morning as the Austrian was accelerating hard past the pits. His rear tyres coated with oil, and he pirouetted straight into the gravel trap at the first corner – to be followed by Bertrand Gachot's Pacific, Eddie Irvine's Jordan, Eric Bernard's Ligier and Michele Alboreto's Minardi.

In the afternoon, both Ferrari drivers used the new 75-degree V12s in first qualifying, but Gerhard pulled off with more engine trouble and Alesi spluttered to a halt out on the circuit low on fuel. But on Saturday, everything came together brilliantly with Berger and Alesi qualifying 1-2 to button up the front row of the grid ahead of Hill's Williams and Schumacher's Benetton. For the first time, both Ferrari drivers would race the new engine.

Despite a multiple collision at the first corner which accounted for no fewer than nine cars, the race was allowed to continue with Berger heading the pack at the end of the opening lap – although Alesi's V12 had broken barely half a mile out of the stadium.

Gerhard was just 0.3sec ahead of Schumacher as he crossed the start/finish line for the first time, the Austrian knowing full well that he was only planning to stop once. Michael, who was stopping twice and thus had a lighter car in the opening stages of the race, tried everything he knew to get past. But Gerhard was in a confident mood and had no intention of relinquishing his advantage in front of the German's home crowd.

On lap 12, Schumacher came in for his first refuelling stop. He resumed fourth, but soon whistled past both Ligiers to retake second place about 22sec behind the Ferrari. On lap 15, Jos Verstappen's Benetton erupted in flames while refuelling in the pit lane, but the blaze was quickly extinguished. The young Dutchman was out on the spot, unhurt apart from a flew flash burns to his face, but four laps later Schumacher began to slow as his Ford V8 unaccountably lost power. At the end of lap 20, with 25 still to run, the German hero was out.

Gerhard now inherited an apparently unassailable advantage. As soon as he was told that Schumacher was slowing, he came in to refuel at the end of lap 20. With the Verstappen conflagration so recently fixed in their minds, the Ferrari crew took a cautious 16.3sec to replenish Gerhard's tank with around 150 litres of Agip. It was more than enough to get him through to the chequered flag.

Despite suffering a pronounced steering vibration in the closing stages, Gerhard had it in the bag. He thought the problem might have been caused by debris on his tyres. 'I pressed hard for two or three laps, trying to clean them up,' he explained. 'Then in the closing stages, I cut back the revs and took things easily.'

He won by almost a minute from Olivier Panis's Ligier. It was a highly emotional victory, ending the longest-ever Ferrari absence from the winner's circle since the team was in at the start of the official World Championship 44 years earlier.

The nicest touch of the afternoon had been the fact that Alesi, for all his tempestuous unpredictability, stayed on the pit wall throughout the race to cheer Gerhard home to victory. 'For me, the race fell into two parts,' explained Jean afterwards. 'The first step was the engine failure, but then I came back to the pits to watch Gerhard's victory unfold.

'I was very nervous, because I felt almost as though I was the team manager and Gerhard was my driver. Sometimes I felt worried. I was following his lap times and they sometimes felt they were too quick, bearing in mind we seemed so close to victory. So I felt very closely involved in the race. I was disappointed to have stopped, of course, but not jealous.'

Unhappily, the Hockenheim success seemed to have been nothing but a brief interlude in the sun. At both Hungaroring and Spa it was a return to dismal disappointment with the team failing to add a single point to its tally. But the long straights at Monza, deep in Ferrari heartland, promised to be different. It could only be helpful that the main man to beat, Michael Schumacher, was banned from competing in both the Italian and Portuguese GPs after he had ignored a black flag at Silverstone.

Both Ferrari drivers were pumped up with a sense of enormous anticipation and stormed round to monopolise the front row of the grid, Alesi taking the first pole position of his career. Then, on race morning, everything began to unravel again. Approaching the Variante Roggia, just after Curva Grande, during the half-hour warm-up session, Gerhard locked his race car's rear brakes and spun heavily into the tyre barrier. It was a substantial impact and everybody held their breath as Berger was lifted from the cockpit and placed on a stretcher at the trackside.

Unbelievably, it took the race officials a full 10 minutes before red flagging the proceedings to a halt. Not only was Gerhard left lying within feet of cars racing by at high speed, but the safety car carrying F1 medical supremo Professor Sid Watkins was prevented from getting to the scene of the accident.

Thankfully, Gerhard was not seriously hurt. He was taken to the circuit medical centre and then on to the nearby Monza hospital where he was found to have strained his neck. He was also acutely frustrated by what he regarded as the chaotic situation at the hospital, but he made it quite clear that, come hell or high water, he was going to return to the circuit and race the spare 412T1B. Bearing in mind that he had already strained his neck in a road accident near the circuit only a few days before the meeting, Berger didn't stint himself when it came to complaining about the situation.

'You cannot leave somebody beside the track like that with cars continuing at 180mph,' he insisted. 'And the guys who removed my helmet need to be shown how to do it, because they just didn't have an idea. Then, when I got to the hospital, there seemed to be 25 doctors pulling me this way and that. One said we need to X-ray this, the other we need to X-ray that. The whole thing was unbelievable, a big casino!'

At the start of the race Alesi accelerated cleanly away ahead of Berger, but as the pack braked for the first chicane, Eddie Irvine's Jordan tapped Johnny Herbert's Lotus into a spin and all hell broke loose with cars scattering in all directions. The race was red-flagged to a halt and everybody had to do it again.

For the second time in an hour Alesi timed his getaway to perfection, completing the opening lap 1.2sec ahead of Berger and the two Williams-Renaults of Hill and Coulthard. Going into the second lap, Gerhard locked up his brakes and straight-lined the sand trap at the first chicane. He was lucky to escape with his Ferrari intact, but this little excursion had the effect of allowing Alesi to open his lead to 3.7sec next time round.

More worryingly, it also dropped Gerhard back into Damon's clutches and the Austrian suffered a great deal of discomfort from his neck in the early part of the race. He had also lost his best engine in the morning's accident, so he concentrated on keeping the Williams at bay while Alesi vanished into the distance.

At the end of lap 14, Jean came in for the first of his two scheduled refuelling stops. The Ferrari was at rest for just 7.8sec, but when Jean went to accelerate back into the fray, the car lurched forward a few yards and stalled. Alesi fiddled with the gearchange paddles. It lurched forward again and stopped.

Without more ado, Jean undid his belts and strode into the Ferrari garage, abandoning his car without as much as a backward glance. Hurling his crash helmet away, he climbed into an Alfa 164 saloon with his brother Jose and drove flat-out all the way back to his home on the Côte d'Azur. Such was his anger that he hurtled straight past the turn-off for Milan's Malpensa airport, ignoring the presence of his own waiting executive jet.

The whole episode was a revealing insight into Alesi's hair-trigger temperament.

Ferrari attempted to pour oil on troubled waters with a soothing official communiqué. The official line was that Jean had returned with transmission problems, that he could not engage first gear and that the Ferrari's gearbox would not select any other gear unless it started in first.

John Barnard rejected this contention out of hand. Alesi, he said, had stripped the dogrings on first gear by selecting the ratio a fraction of a second before first had properly engaged. 'If he had just calmed down, let the revs drop back, and engaged third, he could probably have accelerated back into the race.'

Either way, the Ferrari fans at Monza now had to be content with a single Ferrari running at the head of the field. On lap 24 Berger relinquished first place for a 12.3sec refuelling stop, was briefly balked in the pit lane by Panis's Ligier, and this allowed the

Adoring fans at Monza (LAT).

In 1981, Enzo Ferrari was forced into possibly his most public acknowledgement that the team was not sufficiently abreast of contemporary F1 chassis technology. He therefore decided to recruit former Hesketh, Wolf and Fittipaldi designer Harvey Postlethwaite. The Englishman was given a free hand to develop a totally new chassis to accommodate the team's 120-degree twin turbo 1.5-litre V6 engine for the following season.

Although Postlethwaite personally believed he had sufficient knowledge to embark on a carbon-fibre composite chassis concept, his assessment was that Maranello was not yet equipped to tackle this sort of specialist chassis construction on an 'in house' basis. As a result, Postlethwaite's first chassis was manufactured out of bonded Nomex honeycomb sheet, 'folded' round carbon-fibre composite bulkheads and glued together to produce an exceptionally light, strong structure. Not until the following year would Postlethwaite produce a full carbon-fibre composite chassis, the resultant Ferrari 126C3 making its competition debut in the 1983 British Grand Prix at Silverstone.

Despite this step forward, Ferrari's back-to-back victory in the 1983 Constructors' World Championship was far from the first stage in a mid-1970s style renaissance. In reality, it was more like a slight blip on a gentle decline. In 1984, Michele Alboreto became the first Italian driver to win a Grand Prix at the wheel of a Ferrari since the late Ludovico Scarfiotti triumphed at Monza 18 years earlier.

Williams duo to duck ahead. Gerhard thought he would now have to settle for third, but was surprised to be promoted back to second behind Damon when Coulthard's car ran low on fuel mid-way round the final lap.

The 1994 Italian GP seemed effectively to have marked the end of Ferrari's competitive season. There were a handful of points finishes left – fifth for Gerhard in the European GP at Jerez, third for Alesi at Suzuka, and then a good second for Berger behind Nigel Mansell's Williams at the Australian GP.

In fact, Gerhard should have won that final race at Adelaide, but flat-spotted one set of his race tyres during the race morning warm-up. That meant that he had to change onto a used set at his second refuelling stop, was then baulked by Heinz-Harald Frentzen's Sauber and slipped back to be pressured by Mansell. He slid wide over a kerb on a fast right-hander and Nigel was through to victory. Still, it was a moderately upbeat note on which to round off a season of dramatic ups and downs.

Taken as a whole, it hadn't been a bad race year for Gerhard Berger. The win at Hockenheim had certainly been its highest moment, a symbolic justification of his decision to return to Ferrari at the end of the 1992 season. But the spectre of Ayrton Senna's accident was difficult for Berger to shake off. The loss of his close friend had exacted a profound effect, and no matter how upbeat and cheerful he might outwardly appear, nothing in his Formula 1 career would ever be quite the same again.

Alesi ended the season frustrated with a sixth place in Australia. Schumacher had won the World Championship with 92 points to Hill's 91. Berger was third with 41, and Alesi fifth with 24. But this was his fifth full year in Formula 1 – his 85th race – without a single win. He had kept the faith, tackling each GP with his full impassioned being no matter what the limitations of the car, never given up hope: but victory still eluded him.

Ferrari finished third in the 1994 Constructors' Championship.

Despite appearances the Italian GP seemed effectively to have marked the end of Ferrari's competitive season (LAT).

Chapter Six

The 1995 racing record

From the outset, it was clear that Ferrari's latest tipo 412T2 challenger for 1995 had the potential to be a formidably competitive tool. It was powered by a new 3-litre steel block V12 which could now be positioned further forward in the chassis thanks to the use of the smaller, 140-litre fuel tank permissible under the new regulations. Here was a technical package from Maranello which really looked as though it might surmount the inherent, if marginal, disadvantages involved in retaining this traditional cylinder configuration.

The seven-bearing V12 ran to around 16,500rpm from the outset with generally impressive mechanical reliability. The Maranello engine department, now under the direction of Ing Martinelli's group after the transfer of Claudio Lombardi to the road car side, concentrated as much on developing drivability as out-and-out top-end power.

The 1995 season opened with the Brazilian GP at Interlagos where Renault's superbly reliable V10 engines were now powering new Benetton B195s for Michael Schumacher and Johnny Herbert, in addition to the Williams FW17s handled by Damon Hill and David Coulthard. Berger and Alesi would thus have their work cut out to keep in touch. Yet by the end of second qualifying, both men were well pleased with the way things had developed. They eventually wound up fifth and sixth in the final qualifying order, predictably behind the quartet of Renault-engined machines. But Berger in particular, despite an engine failure in second qualifying, remained bullish. 'I think within another couple of races, we should be able to catch the Williams,' he mused.

At the start, Damon's pole position Williams was just out-gunned by Schumacher's Benetton and the reigning World Champion led the opening lap from Hill, Coulthard, Mika Hakkinen's McLaren-Mercedes and the two Ferraris, Gerhard just ahead of Jean. Hill would eventually get ahead of Schumacher at the first refuelling stop, thereafter edging away into a 3.4sec lead until a left rear suspension failure spun his Williams off the road at the chicane immediately beyond the Interlagos pits.

At the chequered flag, only Schumacher and Coulthard were on the same lap in first and second places. Berger and Alesi were one lap down in third and fifth places, sandwiching Hakkinen's McLaren. The Maranello cars had run reliably enough, but they were down on horsepower.

What happened next propelled Ferrari into the forefront of F1 controversy through no fault of its own. For the 1995 F1 World Championship season, the FIA had developed a rigorous programme of testing for fuel samples, the governing body intent on clamping down on any competitor who might be of a mind to infringe the rules.

On the face of it, the regulations were clear-cut and straightforward. Prior to any specific race, the supplying fuel companies would submit samples from which the FIA

Alesi finished a brilliant second to Hill's Williams in the 1995 Argentinian GP, the first F1 race held in Buenos Aires for 14 years (Allsport).

would make what amounted to a DNA-style 'fingerprint' as a baseline against which any subsequent samples would be checked. If they matched the fingerprint, fine. If they didn't...

Samples of the Elf fuel taken from Coulthard's Williams and Schumacher's Benetton after Friday's first qualifying session were found to be non-approved. Since there was only a single specification Elf fuel available in Brazil, it therefore followed that they were likely to be disqualified from the race.

For whatever reason, Williams and Benetton were only advised of this fuel discrepancy a few minutes before the pit lane opened prior to the start of the race. However, Williams Technical Director Patrick Head and Benetton Managing Director Flavio Briatore were advised by a senior FIA figure that there was no question of disqualifications on the day. The cars raced – and were disqualified. Berger was now promoted to top place on the rostrum, with Alesi third.

FIA President Max Mosley defended the decision to exclude the Renault-engined cars. 'We ran the test which everybody agreed,' he explained. 'Two of the fuel samples – the Agip used by Ferrari and Mobil used by McLaren – matched, and one, Elf, did not. Faced with that eventuality, we had to take action.' Needless to say, Benetton and Williams immediately lodged a formal appeal against the disqualification and an FIA Appeal Court hearing was set for 13 April, four days after the second round of the 1995 World Championship, in Argentina.

Qualifying in Buenos Aires turned out to be a lottery. David Coulthard's Williams took pole position after the Scot found a three-lap spell when the seemingly endless wall of torrential rain eased briefly. As an indication of the dire conditions, David's pole time was almost 23sec slower than the race fastest lap which would be set by Michael Schumacher.

Ferrari fortunes were mixed. Six new revised V12 engines were available, offering enhanced mid-range torque. But although Alesi managed to qualify sixth, Berger was beset by overheating brakes and had to be content with eighth on the grid, one place behind F1 novice Mika Salo's Tyrrell-Yamaha.

The race was red-flagged to a halt after a first corner pile-up in which Alesi was a central player, but his race fortunes were in no way blunted by the need to take the spare car for the restart. In the closing stages, Alesi would mount an increasingly firm challenge to Hill's winning Williams, getting to within 3.8sec of it with just over 20 laps to go.

'Jean was always a worry,' admitted Hill, 'and I wasn't sure I was safe until I was eight seconds ahead with two laps to go.'

Berger finished sixth after a poor start which left him badly bogged down in traffic during the opening stages of the race. He took almost a dozen laps to battle his way ahead of Aguri Suzuki's Ligier and Jos Verstappen's Simtek, running tenth and 11th in the opening stages. He eventually radioed in to report that his 412T2 felt virtually undrivable. At the end of lap 14, believing he had serious damper problems, Gerhard came into the pits where his car was on the point of being pushed back into the garage when Chief Mechanic Nigel Stepney noticed that the right-front tyre was partly deflated.

The car was returned to the race after a massive 81sec delay, resuming 16th. Gerhard spent the remainder of the afternoon battling through to take the final point on offer for sixth place. Ferrari now led the Constructors' Championship with 13 points to the Williams team's 10, and Gerhard was a single point ahead of Hill atop the drivers' table. But all that would be turned on its head during the week which followed.

The FIA Court of Appeal, convening to consider the Brazilian GP disqualifications,

decided to hand back Schumacher and Coulthard their drivers' points gained for first and second places in the race, while at the same time fining Benetton and Williams each $200,000, as well as withdrawing the Constructors' Championship points accruing to the two cars from that race.

The Appeal Court heard Elf accept the fact that there was a 'quantitative difference' between the Elf fuel homologated with the FIA and that used in Brazil. Elf maintained that this error – which amounted to an administrative discrepancy – offered no measurable performance advantage. Indeed Hill used the same fuel, by now officially registered, to win quite legally in Buenos Aires. It was also believed that evidence submitted by Elf, indicating possible variations between fuel test results produced by different makes of gas chromatograph – the machine which checks the fuel samples – was a significant factor considered by the Appeal Court members.

Officially, Ferrari kept its own counsel on the matter. But Niki Lauda delivered a

Such a famous name, such a famous symbol. But how long would it be before the Prancing Horse galloped to another World Championship victory (Allsport)?

113

Gerhard Berger on his way to third place in the San Marino GP at Imola, a race he might have won had he not stalled during a routine pit stop (Allsport).

blistering assault on the governing body, published in the Austrian newspaper *Salzburger Nachrichten*. It was difficult to imagine that his views did not have the tacit blessing of the Maranello top brass. Lauda didn't pull any punches, accusing the FIA of being unable to govern Formula 1 properly and in an appropriate manner.

'The verdict is the greatest joke of all time,' he said. 'I cannot separate car and driver completely. If this is the new rule, that you can build an illegal car and let the team pay

for victory, the whole thing is only commercial and has nothing to do with sport any more. The next time, we could build a car with a five-litre engine, win and pay. It's like scoring a half goal in soccer – it's just not possible. Either you score a goal, or not. The decision for me is the biggest defeat for the FIA who cannot govern the sport any longer.'

The Ferrari press office followed this up with a terse statement which could be taken to endorse Lauda's somewhat colourful language: 'The decisions made successively by the FIA International Court of Appeal seem to imply – from now on – a driver may win a Grand Prix even if racing with a car that is not complying with the technical regulations.'

The previous weekend, Ferrari President Luca di Montezemolo had appeared in the pit lane at Buenos Aires, 21 years to the race after Niki Lauda and Clay Regazzoni finished second and third in the Argentinian GP to begin Maranello's 1974 renaissance. He could see the irony of that anniversary. In reality, he was in exactly the same situation: trying to revive the Prancing Horse as a consistent Grand Prix winning force.

Yet Montezemolo firmly expressed his belief that Ferrari could once again scale the Big Time. 'I feel now, around Ferrari, a sense of interest and attention. I am aware of gigantic support for Ferrari. OK, so you ask me when can Ferrari win the championship again? Well, I say to you that if we can make the same improvement in 1995 as we did last year, then next year, to be honest, I think we will be ready.

'But it is important to emphasize that, effectively, three years ago we were started more or less from zero, with what amounted to a new team. I think the three or four years before Enzo Ferrari died, and the period immediately after his death, represented the worst time for the company. There were too many people around with insufficient experience and without a clear number one in charge.' That, he insists, has all changed. 'Operating this team efficiently is a question of organisation and mentality, and I believe that Jean Todt had this under control.'

Such flattery, however, didn't prevent the team's Sporting Director from softening Montezemolo's optimism about winning the title in 1996. 'I think 1997 is more realistic,' said Todt. 'We know better than our rivals which point we have now reached,

115

where we are coming from. It is that last 10 per cent of performance which is the most demanding in terms of finance. We are competing with Renault, Mercedes-Benz and Peugeot. They have bigger budgets and more people.'

After the two South American races, Maranello lined up for what was, emotionally at least, its most important single race of the season. Many Ferrari fans may regard the Italian GP at Monza as an occasion for mass ritual obeisance, but the San Marino event at Imola is closer to the marque's heartland, both geographically and emotionally.

To start with the Imola circuit, just off the Bologna to Rimini autostrada, is named the Autodromo Enzo e Dino Ferrari. It is also widely regarded as providing a slightly more tranquil, easy-going environment in which the *Ferrariste* parade their passionate enthusiasm. Whereas the frenzy of the fans at Monza sometimes assumes an unattractively aggressive edge, the mood seems to soften slightly once they get away from the fringes of metropolitan Milan.

Of course, the 1995 San Marino race was a moment of symbolic renewal for the F1 fraternity. The 1994 event had been blighted by the deaths of rookie Simtek driver Roland Ratzenberger in practice, and then of Ayrton Senna when his Williams FW16 crashed while leading in the early stages. These deaths had a far-reaching effect on the Grand Prix community. In particular, Gerhard Berger had seriously considered retiring. Yet the popular Austrian shrugged aside his inner doubts, deciding to continue in his chosen sport, and when he lined up to do battle at Imola in 1995, he could genuinely be regarded as a potential winner.

For the San Marino race, Maranello produced two examples of a revised engine specification, the strategy being that the slightly more powerful 'update' would be installed for Alesi and Berger to use only in second qualifying. Unfortunately, Gerhard's original V12 developed a problem shortly after it was installed on the Thursday afternoon, so he had to switch to the more powerful unit right from the outset.

Again, Ferrari's technical package looked pretty impressive. Gerhard was able to get within 0.008sec of Michael Schumacher's provisional pole position time in the Benetton B195 on the first day, a particularly noteworthy achievement bearing in mind the fact that both Williams and Benetton had the uprated Renault RS7 V10 available for the first time at this race. It also provided worthwhile copy for the gossip-hungry local media, for Gerhard had recently exchanged stern words with his German colleague over the question of his Brazilian GP disqualification and reinstatement.

On Friday night the track was doused with a heavy shower, washing away much of the rubber laid the previous day which ensured that the front row times would not be matched in second qualifying. Gerhard quickly concluded that there was no realistic chance of bettering his own time, so set off to scrub in some fresh rubber in preparation for the following day's race.

Meanwhile, both Hill and Coulthard were right on the pace and Berger suddenly got a message over his radio link that the young Scot had taken pole position. He piled on the pressure – and slid off briefly at the Tamburello chicane, now redesigned to make it safer – returning to the pits feeling slightly annoyed after being told that the initial message was a mistake. Alesi remained in fifth place on the grid, also failing to improve on his Friday best, separated from Berger by the Williams FW17 duo, Coulthard and Hill.

As things transpired, all the tactical decisions which affected the race's outcome were taken in the aftermath of the saturated warm-up session on Sunday morning. Alesi and Berger topped the timing sheets, but although the rain had abated before the start, the circuit still glistened ominously. Now it was a question of whether or not to start on slicks in the hope that the racing line would quickly dry out, or opt for rain tyres with the prospect of having to make an early first pit stop.

San Marino, 1995, and a moment of symbolic renewal. Both Alesi and Berger had a place with winner Damon Hill on the podium (ICN UK Bureau).

Both Ferrari and Williams drivers, plus Schumacher and Jordan-Peugeot's Rubens Barrichello decided on the latter course. It was the right way to go. From the start, Schumacher accelerated cleanly into an immediate lead from Berger, Coulthard and Hill, Gerhard completing the opening lap only 0.7sec behind the Benetton.

It took just five laps before the leaders were in among the slick-shod backmarkers. Berger, who had sat thoughtfully behind Michael as the World Champion wrestled with his precarious-looking Benetton, got badly held up by Luca Badoer's Minardi which had unfortunately shed one of its rear-view mirrors on the opening lap. But the track seemed to be drying steadily now, so Berger came in for an 8.8sec tyre and refuelling stop at the end of lap six, briefly dropping back to fifth.

At the end of his ninth lap, Schumacher also made for the pit lanes and a change to slicks. Hill followed him in, and when Coulthard stopped two laps later, Michael seemed on course to regain the lead. However, he pushed too hard on cold slicks and crashed heavily after hitting a puddle on the approach to the second Piratella left-hander. This left Gerhard leading comfortably ahead of Hill and Coulthard, the Williams duo now closely shadowed by Alesi.

Watching brief. Alesi and Berger, contemplating life together in what would prove to be the last season at Maranello for both of them (LAT).

On the face of it, the Williams was still the quickest car on the circuit, but the leading bunch was having a more than usually difficult time picking a path through the slower competitors, so Berger was operating from a position of strength. Unfortunately, he then stalled as he made to restart from his second refuelling stop at the end of lap 22.

'During the warm-up, I had been worried about the feel of the hand clutch and the engine just stalled when I was in for the second time,' he shrugged. 'That lost me all chance of competing for a position at the front. I think the Williams-Renaults were still more competitive, but we might have had a chance.'

Damon thus went through into a lead he was never to relinquish, leaving Alesi to come home second ahead of the disappointed Berger. Jean rounded off the day with some righteous indignation about Coulthard's driving tactics, accusing the Scot of deliberately driving into him as they braked for the downhill Rivazza left-hander, and of adopting 'incorrect' tactics. Coulthard was nonplussed. 'I always deal with these

Alesi at Monaco where he was quickest in the first timed session, but retired after crashing with Martin Brundle (Allsport).

things in a private way,' he said. 'If Jean has a problem, I'm sure like a nice man he'll come along and square it with me.' The episode fizzled out.

For Berger, it was a particularly frustrating weekend, off the track as well as on – he'd watched as his Testa Rossa road car was stolen from outside the local Molino Rosso hotel, before his very eyes on Friday evening. 'I was walking to my car because I wanted to go out for dinner. When I was about 20 metres away I could see the car being moved out of the parking space.

'I said to myself "they want to move my car – maybe it was in the way". So I kept walking. And then I thought "but how can they move my car if the key is in my hand?" I went right into the middle of the road to stop it, but the guy tried to run over me and I jumped out of the way. I ran behind and tried to open the door, but he'd locked it from the inside and went through a gap between some other parked cars by what seemed a fraction of a centimetre. So the car is stolen!'

Lapping the slower cars: Berger comes up behind a Ligier and Tyrrell in Canada (LAT).

Next stop was Barcelona's Circuit de Catalunya where both 412T2s looked strong from the outset. Alesi and Berger so convincingly out-ran their rivals in Friday's first qualifying that Gerhard was moved to offer a word of caution to the fans.

'I must admit that I'm a bit surprised at this result,' he confessed. 'I still feel that, especially in race trim, we are not yet at the level of our strongest opponents.' He was right. After making some significant overnight chassis set-up changes, Schumacher's Benetton blitzed its way to pole position and then ran away with the race.

Alesi qualified second ahead of Gerhard and held second place in the opening stages. But Berger had noticed that his team-mate's car was spewing out coolant from the start of the parade lap and doubted he would survive. He was right. Despite emerging from his first refuelling stop still second ahead of Hill's Williams, Alesi's Ferrari had a major engine failure at the end of lap 25.

With Hill dropping from second to fourth on the final lap, his Williams suffering from a hydraulic problem which caused the throttle mechanism to pack up two corners from home, Berger was able to get home third behind a Schumacher-Johnny Herbert Benetton 1-2.

'To be honest, I wasn't very happy how I drove the race,' admitted Gerhard. 'I had a bad start and couldn't get things quite right. I didn't really know whether two or three stops was the right strategy and I seemed to be on the radio to the pit all the time. As it was, we did three stops, but I think we should have only made two.'

As the F1 circus moved on to Monaco, Schumacher was now topping the Drivers' Championship one point ahead of Hill, with Alesi and Berger trailing third and fourth.

In first qualifying through the streets of the Principality, Alesi displayed dazzling form to edge out Schumacher for fastest time by 0.39sec. He twice kissed the guard rails in the process, but insisted it was no problem. Gerhard was also in terrific form, hurtling out of Casino Square in great opposite-lock slides to finish the day a confident third. Then, in second qualifying, it all went wrong for Maranello.

The Saturday session had started with a brilliant set-to between Schumacher and Hill, but Alesi was confident he could retain fastest time and duly accelerated out to put his Renault-engined rivals in their place. Unfortunately his Ferrari rolled to a halt at Rascasse, just before the pit entrance, due to a problem with the hydraulic pressure to the semi-automatic gearchange mechanism. He received a push-start from some marshals, enabling him to get back into the pit lane, but that was a clear breach of the rules.

The stewards decided to ban him from using his race car for the balance of the session. Thus the dejected Jean mooched around waiting for Berger to finish with his own car – and the team effectively put unnecessary pressure on Gerhard to hurry through his runs more quickly than he would have liked. Berger couldn't improve on fourth before relinquishing his car to Alesi, the Ferrari mechanics working like dervishes to change the pedal positions as the minutes ticked away.

Alesi, remarkably under control, then tore into his final lap only 13sec before the chequered flag fell. It was a hopeless, if gallant, quest which ended with fifth place in the final grid order.

Alesi on the rostrum after his memorable first victory at the 1995 Canadian GP. Rubens Barrichello and Eddie Irvine, respectively second and third for Jordan, share the celebrations (ICN UK Bureau).

'Believed media rather than drivers'

In 1985, Maranello bounced back into contention with Alboreto winning the Canadian and German Grands Prix, leading the World Championship points table ahead of the McLaren-mounted Alain Prost after the latter event. 'Prost had a better car than me that day, so it was good to be able to stay in front,' commented Michele after his success at the new Nurburgring.

Thereafter, Ferrari's challenge collapsed like a house of cards. Many people felt that Maranello's lack of an in-house wind tunnel was responsible for the inconsistent handling from the type 156 chassis, but Alboreto would always reflect that the key deficiency throughout 1985 was insufficient engine power. That, and the team's notoriously exaggerated regard for the Italian media which, on many occasions, seemed to be steering the company's racing fortunes more forcefully than did the Maranello management.

'The media in Italy are capable of convincing the Ferrari management about any aspect of the car's performance,' recalled an exasperated Alboreto. 'And they, in turn, are prepared to believe the media far more than the drivers.

Throughout the 1984 and 1985 seasons we kept saying we hadn't got enough power, but then some newspaper would come up with a statistic that we had the fastest speed in a straight line at some circuit or other.

'Then we would have to try explaining that the reason we were quick on the straight was because we were running no wing, and that the driveability of the engine was poor because there was (virtually) no power at the bottom of the rev range.'

Having squandered a very genuine chance of tilting at the World Championship in 1985, Ferrari fortunes continued to fade through into 1986. The team was acutely frustrated, but seemed adrift and lacking in focused management capability. Enzo Ferrari himself was now frail and ageing, although still with almost two more years to live and, nominally at least, in complete control of the racing team which carried his name.

Nevertheless, Fiat president Vittorio Ghidella was now acutely concerned about the team's indifferent and patchy performances. Momentous decisions would have to be made if Ferrari was to be steered away from imminent disaster.

There was worse to come. On the sprint to Ste Devote on the opening lap, Alesi came storming up the inside from his third row starting position to make it three abreast with Berger and Coulthard as they aimed for the first turn. As the right-hand guard rail squeezes the track width on the approach to the corner, Jean found his left front wheel brushing Coulthard's right-hand side pod.

Suddenly David was vaulting over Alesi's left front wheel, spinning violently in front of the pack after bouncing into Berger. Both Ferraris were left stalled in the middle of the corner and the race was red-flagged to a halt. Fortunately, Maranello's strategy of bringing two spare cars along to this potentially tricky event was now fully vindicated, allowing both Alesi and Berger to take the restart in back-up cars.

At the end of the day Schumacher won from Hill, with Gerhard coming out of the event with another third place. Alesi, meanwhile, briefly led on lap 37 before making his own single refuelling stop to get back in the race ahead of Damon. His great charge finished ignominiously in the barrier at Tabac after 42 of the race's 78 laps, Alesi trying to avoid Martin Brundle's spinning Ligier which had held him up for several laps, although it was a lap behind the Ferrari.

'Despite being shown the blue flags, Brundle was driving so much on the limit to

Previous pages: Joy for Alesi in Canada (LAT). Right: Jean Todt keeps a close eye. All agree that he exerted an often much-needed calming influence at race weekends (LAT).

block me that he eventually touched the guard rail and spun in front of me,' fumed Jean. Brundle simply replied that he had his own agenda and the incident had not been his fault.

Berger emerged from the race in a slightly more philosophical frame of mind. 'I was a bit unlucky,' he explained. 'I had a good start and thought "I'll be third going into the first corner". Suddenly I just saw the front wing of the car spinning next to me – Coulthard – and crashing into my car. Unfortunately Coulthard and Alesi touched each other and spun into my car.

'This was very bad for me, because I had to switch to my T-car which was the only chassis of the four fitted with an older specification engine. It was down on power, but the rest of the race was fine. I had a two-stop strategy, but I think Michael's strategy of one stop was right. I was a bit stuck behind Johnny Herbert after my first stop, so I couldn't capitalise on the use of that fresh rubber. But I'm happy with third place and I'm now third in the championship.'

Next on the agenda was the Canadian GP at Montreal, traditionally one of the longest races on the calendar at 189.934 miles (69 laps) and extremely marginal on fuel consumption. Schumacher qualified his Benetton on pole from Hill, Coulthard, Berger and Alesi and, with Maranello opting for a single refuelling stop for both cars, it was decided that whichever of the V12s was best placed coming up to the half distance mark would stop on lap 34, his team-mate a lap later.

Gerhard got a good start to complete the opening lap in fourth place behind Coulthard, but on the second lap the Scot spun wildly approaching a right-hander on the return leg of the circuit. Gerhard backed off momentarily and Jean nipped ahead. They now settled down to run in that order, both men eventually wearing down Hill's ill-handling Williams to move ahead into second and third places.

On lap 34, Alesi duly made his refuelling stop, allowing Gerhard through into second place. But the Austrian quickly discovered just how close to the bone his V12 was running in terms of fuel consumption. Before he could come in one lap later, his Ferrari began stuttering with pick-up problems and he could only limp into the pit lane at little more than walking pace, trailing back into the contest a bitterly disappointed eighth. The fact that his problem had been exacerbated by a fault with the cockpit instrument display was scant consolation.

On lap 38, Schumacher was sufficiently far ahead of Alesi to make a scheduled 12.9sec single refuelling stop and emerge with his lead intact. With Hill retiring on lap 51 with another Williams hydraulic failure, the Benetton team leader stood poised dramatically to extend his championship advantage. Then suddenly it all went wrong. On lap 58, Schumacher slowed dramatically as his car refused to shift out of third gear. As he made for the pits, Alesi surged confidently into the lead.

'I had been running second when, suddenly, as I came out of the last hairpin, I saw Schumacher's car on the big television screen,' recounted Jean. 'He was in the pits and they were taking off the steering wheel. I hardly dared to hope, but then the team came on the radio and told me he was out.

'With 10 laps to go, I knew I could win and I started to cry in the car. Every time I braked, my tears were hitting the visor. For about a lap, I felt a bit disorientated, but then said to myself "now you have to get back to driving" and after that I was OK.'

In fact, Schumacher was not totally out of the equation. The glitch in his Benetton's gearchange system was rectified and he tore back into the fray, eventually to finish fifth. But by then Alesi had taken the chequered flag. This was his first Formula 1 victory after competing in 91 grands prix, one of the longest apprenticeships in the history of the sport, and it came on his 31st birthday.

Fifth place was the best Alesi could manage at the 1995 French GP at Magny-Cours (Allsport).

For the Canadian crowd the sight of a Ferrari carrying the familiar number 27 so closely identified with their national hero Gilles Villeneuve – and on a circuit bearing his name – it was too much to contain. They erupted over the barriers and flooded onto the circuit at the start/finish line.

Meanwhile, Berger could also have been forgiven for wiping a tear from his eye. Yet it would have been from frustration rather than joy. Five laps from the finish, he came to the end of his tether and barged Martin Brundle's Ligier off the road as they battled for sixth place and the final championship points of the day. 'I got two wheels on the grass and couldn't brake any more,' he offered by way of explanation. 'This has been a very bad day for me.'

With neither Williams finishing, and Schumacher delayed, Ferrari now vaulted from third place into the lead of the Constructors' Championship. This set people thinking that perhaps Maranello had turned the corner. But it hadn't. Like Hockenheim the year before, the Canadian victory was just a brief interlude in the sun.

For the next race, the F1 fraternity moved back across the Atlantic to the billiard smooth surface of the Circuit de Nevers at Magny-Cours. Yet if the Ferraris had hoped to be front-running contenders, their V12 performance was increasingly eclipsed by the advent of a further up-rated Renault RS7B V10 available to both Benetton and Williams at this race.

Alesi and Berger qualified fourth and seventh, reflecting a frustrating level of mechanical unreliability in the run-up to the race. Jean lost virtually the entire Saturday morning session when his car rolled to a halt with gearchange hydraulic pump failure. As a result, the chassis set-up wasn't sufficiently polished in second qualifying and he remained 1.5sec shy of Hill's pole-winning best.

Gerhard's 412T2 had to be rebuilt round a fresh monocoque after he'd kerbed it heavily on Friday. Then he lost time with a hydraulic system leak on Saturday morning. 'No set-up, no good lap,' he explained ruefully.

The exuberant Alesi pitched Herbert's Benetton into a spin only three laps into the race as the two men jousted for sixth. After that Jean simply existed in the race, slogging home an off-the-pace fifth. Gerhard briefly made it through to third place before his first refuelling stop on lap 22. The nozzle on the refuelling hose initially refused to engage and he was stationary for almost a minute before resuming 17th. He climbed back to 12th at the chequered flag after another Sunday afternoon he would prefer to forget.

Benetton was now back ahead in the battle for Constructors' title points, but Maranello was upbeat about its prospects for the British GP at Silverstone, the season's halfway point. However, despite some aerodynamic revisions to the side pods and diffusers, Berger and Alesi found that lack of testing at Silverstone posed something of a problem. Gerhard lined up fourth behind Schumacher, Hill and Coulthard, with Jean sixth on the inside of the third row alongside Herbert.

Gerhard blew his advantage at the start, coming round eighth on the opening lap, but Alesi made a barnstorming dragster of a getaway to rocket straight through into second place behind Hill's Williams on the sprint down to Copse corner on the opening lap. That enabled Damon to make good his escape, the Englishman delighted that Jean was left to box in Schumacher for the opening phase of the battle.

Gerhard fought through to fifth before making his first refuelling stop 20 laps into the 61-lap race. Yet more frustration. The left front wheel was not properly secured, causing him to wobble to a halt mid-way round his next lap. He was left with no choice but to abandon an otherwise healthy car at the side of the circuit and begin the long walk back to the paddock.

After losing the lead to Schumacher at his second refuelling stop, Hill then became embroiled in a controversial collision with his Benetton rival, eliminating both cars from the race. Logically, Alesi should by now have been in a position to inherit the lead, but his performance had faded dramatically to the point where he dropped back to take second at the chequered flag behind an exultant Johnny Herbert, all fired up to achieve his first GP win. With the V12's oil pressure dwindling in the closing stages, Jean was told to roll it off and be satisfied with three championship points. It was difficult to see why.

In retrospect, for both Ferrari drivers, Silverstone 1995 could be regarded as a turning point. Almost imperceptibly, there was a shift of mood within the Italian camp. The relationship between F1 teams and their drivers is always a delicately balanced affair, none more so than at Ferrari. Old traditions die hard at Maranello. Approbation from the management can mean celebrity status, but if the tide turns against you, this can quickly be transformed into disapproval as relentless as a thumbs-down from the Emperor at the Forum.

Alesi was always going to be the most vulnerable. Although dynamically talented, he invariably displayed a hair-trigger temperament. Ken Tyrrell had sought to soften these asperities during his F1 apprenticeship, but the volatility was always there, lurking just beneath the surface. Had he gone to Williams in 1991, life might have been very different for both parties. In many ways, Ferrari – extremely daunting for any young driver still proving himself – was the last place on earth where Alesi's talent would flourish.

That Canadian victory had, however, given Jean a heady taste for the winner's champagne. Then suddenly, Luca di Montezemolo began displaying an almost embarrassingly uninhibited enthusiasm for both Michael Schumacher and Damon Hill as possible candidates for his 1996 driver line-up. To publicly flaunt his negotiating hand so early in the season seemed calculated to do nothing but undermine the confidence of Ferrari's existing drivers.

So it proved. Speaking to the Italian newspaper *La Stampa*, the Ferrari supremo was quoted as saying: 'To win in Formula 1, you need three things – a good organisation, a great car and a great driver. In my role as President, I have to bring home the best. Schumacher is undoubtedly the best and I have a duty to think of him.

'We are likely to have a decision by mid-August. But I have been talking not only to Schumacher, but with others as well. With Hill, for example – a very serious type and decidedly faster than he appears to be.' In fact, Damon had been approached as early as the Spanish GP, barely a fortnight after Ferrari emissary Niki Lauda had made contact with Eddie Irvine's personal manager, the British former journalist Mike Greasley. The Prancing Horse seemed determined to trip itself up badly even before the European leg of the 1995 season was seriously underway.

The reality, of course, was as stark as it was straightforward. Montezemolo didn't have to be a genius to appreciate the obvious and uncomfortable truth. Neither Alesi nor Berger were quite capable of taking Ferrari that final mile to a World Championship. Fine drivers both, but not in the absolute top rank. Montezemolo was playing for high stakes. And with Ayrton Senna now dead, that meant Michael Schumacher.

The Philip Morris cigarette conglomerate, via its Marlboro brand, was prepared to chip in with a major contribution to help Ferrari make Schumacher a financial offer he couldn't refuse. In addition, there was the promise of yet another good chassis from John Barnard's design team and the abandonment of Maranello's V12 engine in favour of an all-new V10. For his part, Schumacher considered the matter carefully. There was no hurry; the World Champion held all the negotiating cards.

More ominously, in the run-up to the German GP at Hockenheim, Montezemolo had also effectively signalled that Alesi would be leaving the team at the end of the year. 'Alesi has been very clear,' he noted. 'He has said that the German's presence is not compatible with him. Alesi knows how much I admire him. But I have told him this and I say it again: it is important not to make accusations about treachery and not to behave like a little baby.'

Nevertheless, Berger came to Hockenheim hoping for a repeat of his 1994 victory. After three days of development work with test driver Nicola Larini at Imola, he was confident that the 412T2 had a good aerodynamic set-up for this race. He qualified a strong fourth, but Alesi ran too much downforce in qualifying and lined up a disappointed tenth. Already, so it seemed, he was being marginalised within the Ferrari organisation.

Come the race, Gerhard drove as well as he'd done the previous year, but he was amazed to find himself flagged in for a 10sec stop-go penalty at the end of the fifth lap, allegedly for jumping the start. 'I am sure my car was still behind the line when the green light came on,' he complained. 'I was told that when I put it into first gear, the car moved only seven centimetres, but I was still penalised. I think the electronic control system (which identified the jump start) is too sensitive.'

He stormed back from 14th to an eventual third at the chequered flag, but Alesi was an early retirement with engine failure. Ferrari emerged from the race holding onto

second place in the Constructors' points table by a single point ahead of Williams. Maranello's 1995 fortunes were now on the slide.

Behind the scenes, the days were ticking away to confirmation of Michael Schumacher's deal with Ferrari.

In first qualifying for the Hungarian GP at the tortuous Hungaroring, Jean Alesi looked wayward from the outset and finally crashed heavily. He was taken to hospital for a routine check-up, but escaped with mild whiplash effect and was back in the cockpit the following day. He qualified sixth and suffered another engine failure in the race.

Berger fared slightly better, taking yet another third place. It was a busy race for the Austrian who spent much of the afternoon grappling with understeer after losing a front wing end-plate when he tapped Luca Badoer's Minardi while lapping the slower machine. Running fourth in the closing stages, he had his hands and mirrors full of Herbert's Benetton and Heinz-Harald Frentzen's Sauber-Ford, but was elevated to a place on the podium when Rubens Barrichello's Jordan-Peugeot suffered engine failure and slowed to a crawl coming out of the very last corner of the final lap.

Then came the Big News. In the week immediately following the Hungarian GP, Ferrari officially confirmed that Michael Schumacher had signed a two-year deal to lead the team in 1996 and 1997. Although this information was contained in a brisk three-line communiqué from Maranello, it looked set to ensure that the 26-year-old German ace became the highest paid driver in F1 history.

Above: Gerhard speeds to third place at the Hungarian GP, beaten by the Williams-Renaults of Hill and Coulthard (LAT). Right: Getting ready. Alesi slides into the cockpit for the Italian GP at Monza (LAT).

Schumacher's $25 million guaranteed minimum income for 1996 would be made up of a $20 million retainer supplemented by patches on his helmet and overalls from Dekra, the German road car testing chain which had already backed him for several years, to the tune of another $5 million's worth of personal sponsorship. Financial support for Ferrari's most lavish driver bid ever had come from Marlboro and Shell, the latter set to resume its association as the team's fuel and oil sponsor, replacing Agip.

Some observers regarded Shell's return to F1 as potentially indiscreet at a time when the multi-national oil company was laying off staff in some departments, but there was a hard commercial edge to its decision. Apart from the obvious benefits of an association with Ferrari, both from an image and a fuel technology standpoint, Shell was facing a PR disaster in Germany over its plans to dispose of the redundant *Brent Spar* oil rig by sinking it deep in the Atlantic ocean.

With the Green movement particularly active in German politics, Shell experienced something of a rough ride for a couple of months during the summer of 1995 with several of its petrol stations being attacked. Linking with Germany's great sporting hero Michael Schumacher could be regarded as nothing if not an absolutely positive development under the circumstances.

Schumacher's 1996 contract called for absolute number one status and priority access to all the latest technical resources and equipment. The implications of the deal were neatly summed up by Fiat boss Gianni Agnelli: 'When you have a driver like Schumacher, if you don't win, it's the team's fault.' In fact it was a no-lose package for the German – because of he did win, he would doubtless expect to take the credit.

As for the Philip Morris cigarette conglomerate, the forging of this spectacular new partnership was widely regarded as representing the absolute pinnacle of the career of Marlboro's sponsorship mastermind John Hogan. Marlboro's colours had first been carried in F1 by the long-defunct BRM team back in 1972 at a time when nobody was quite certain how to get the best 'bang for the buck' from commercial motor racing sponsorship.

The Marlboro BRM alliance had been uncomfortable and uneasy. It ended in 1973 and Marlboro switched its colours to McLaren at the start of the following year. Hogan became one of the key figures behind Marlboro's continuing F1 involvement. He helped recruit James Hunt for McLaren at the start of 1976 following the departure of double World Champion Emerson Fittipaldi. Hogan was as astute and knowledgeable about the business world as he was about motor racing. There have been few such overwhelmingly influential people in the sport to combine those qualities.

Despite being extremely satisfied with its McLaren partnership, Philip Morris was keen to become identified with Ferrari. That seemed to be out of the question in the mid-1970s when Enzo Ferrari, still hale and hearty, dismissed the idea out of hand. The Maranello patriarch clung to the somewhat lofty viewpoint that his cars did not run on cigarette tobacco. It was an idealistic notion which continued to find favour with the purists, but as Ferrari's F1 team rolled on into the 1980s, so costs began to spiral. And Marlboro kept wooing him.

Eventually, the Commendatore gave way. The transition to the era of Marlboro-backed Ferrari F1 cars was engineered by a deal simply to contribute to the drivers' retainers from 1984 onwards. Identification on the cars themselves was minimal. But it took only a few years for that to accelerate into a full-blown sponsorship arrangement with lavish Marlboro billing on the engine cover, front bodywork and rear wing. It was another triumph for John Hogan's cajoling.

By the start of the 1996 season, Marlboro was beginning its 23rd unbroken year as the McLaren team's title sponsor. But asked what the outcome might be if Marlboro

Hats off to the Ferrari concession stand at Monza for covering most options (LAT).

Ferrari enthusiasts get everywhere (LAT).

had to choose between one team or the other, Hogan was in no doubt whatsoever. It would be Ferrari every time.

'We know exactly what we get out of our Formula 1 involvement and, better than any other sponsor, we know how to capitalise on it,' noted Hogan enigmatically. Clinching the services of Michael Schumacher, the man poised to become the highest paid sportsman in the world and undoubtedly the best Grand Prix driver of his era, may have been a mind-numbing expense for Philip Morris. But nobody was even vaguely suggesting that it wasn't worth the effort and investment.

Meanwhile, Damon Hill renewed his Williams contract for 1996 in the wake of a commanding victory at the Hungaroring. His battle for the 1995 title then continued at Spa where Berger and Alesi neatly buttoned up the front row by the simple expedient of being out on the

Montezemolo cut through the charade

Born in Bologna on 31 August 1947, Luca Cordero di Montezemolo had graduated in law from Rome University in 1971 and subsequently specialised in commercial law at New York's Columbia University. During this period he toyed with the idea of competition driving and was briefly involved in the Lancia rally team before completing his legal studies.

His introduction to the Fiat empire came through a close friend who was a nephew of Fiat overlord Gianni Agnelli. In June 1973 Luca was appointed as Enzo Ferrari's personal assistant – the Commendatore's eyes and ears at the races – and manager of the racing department as the F1 team attempted to dig itself out of the depressing performance rut it was floundering in by the start of that season.

In 1992 it was a measure of Montezemolo's status that even dyed-in-the-wool sceptics believed that, as Ferrari President, he had a better than evens chance of reviving the F1 fortunes of the Prancing Horse. After all, hadn't he presided over Ferrari's resurgence in the mid-1970s, building the platform from which Niki Lauda had won his first World Championship for the team in 1975?

Luca's new job as President was estimated to be worth at least £300,000 a year, but this scion of a wealthy family wasn't doing it for money. Lean, athletic and with the looks of a movie star, Luca wasn't short of a lire. He had dramatically embellished his CV in the interval since his first stint at Maranello.

After leaving in 1976, he became Director of External Relations for the Fiat Group until 1981 when he took a year off to fill the role as manager for Operation *Azzurra*, the first Italian boat to enter the America's Cup race. Later that same year he became Managing Director of ITEDI SpA, the holding company which co-ordinates all the publishing activities of the Fiat Group, including *La Stampa*, the second most popular daily newspaper in Italy.

At the end of 1983 he made another career change, being appointed as Managing Director of Cinzano International SpA, a further offshoot of the Fiat empire. Then from 1985–90 he was the high-profile Director General of the Organising Committee for Italia '90, his country's hosting of the World Cup. Once that enormous task was completed, Luca took over as Managing Director of RCS Video, an influential media group whose interests included the top newspaper, *Corriera della Sera*.

Yet, for all this achievement, ever since Enzo Ferrari's death in August 1988, there had been a feeling that Luca was somehow the annointed, logical successor to head up the most famous motor racing company in the world. And so it came to pass.

Soon after Luca's succession, Niki Lauda – who had won two of his three World Championships in a Ferrari – would be taken aboard as a consultant to the F1 team. On the face of it, the old colleagues had taken up where they had left off in 1976. Reflecting on those earlier days together, Niki remarked: 'Once I got to know Luca, I quickly realised how valuable his contribution was over the winter of 1973–74, just before I joined Ferrari as a driver.

'He was very good at telling the Old Man precisely what was happening out on the circuits. Also, he did that with a totally impartial mind, which was very good because maybe the lines of communication hadn't been too good before.' In making this remark, Lauda was certainly drawing not only on his English fluency, but also his remarkable capacity for ironic understatement!

Before Luca's first stint with the organisation, Ferrari's F1 team managers had traditionally reported whatever the Commendatore had wanted to hear. Or, at least, what they judged he wanted to hear. Isolated in his Maranello fortress, never travelling to the races, he had become vulnerable to biased titbits of information which were designed to reflect well on the team managers, less so on the drivers. Factions and strife soon developed as a direct result of this strategy. Montezemolo cut through the charade. He had no axe to grind and, benefiting from Agnelli's patronage, no inclination to distort the facts when reporting to his boss.

Now he was back at the helm of the entire Ferrari company. But no matter how much enthusiasm and commitment he would bring to bear on the problem, it would take time before the Maranello ship would respond to the new captain at the helm and swing away from its seemingly inevitable collision course with disaster.

circuit for the handful of laps when the surface was actually dry in both qualifying sessions.

Sadly, the race was a disaster for Ferrari. Alesi led the second lap from Herbert's Benetton, but was in the pits complaining about poor handling at the end of lap four. The scarlet machine was fitted with a set of fresh tyres, Jean accelerated back into the race only to pull off immediately a few yards after the pit exit. His mount had suffered a suspension breakage. Gerhard fared little better, being delayed by a persistent misfire which failed to respond to a change of the engine's electronic control unit. He eventually called it a day after 22 of the race's 44 laps.

Ferrari's drivers might have been forgiven had they gone into the Italian GP at Monza in a dejected frame of mind – but turning out for the team at this motorsport shrine seemed to galvanise them to try to prove that Maranello had made the wrong decision in terms of its 1996 driver arrangements.

In the run-up to the Monza race, the clever money in the F1 paddock still had Gerhard Berger firmly in place as Schumacher's team-mate for the following year. True, Berger had made some critical remarks about Schumacher prior to the Belgian GP, but this had been widely interpreted simply as a means of flushing out precisely where he stood in relation to Todt and Montezemolo as far as the proposed terms of his 1996 contract were concerned.

In the immediate aftermath of Schumacher's official signing, the speculation about the German driver's priority in the team had left Gerhard feeling particularly nettled. He immediately fired back to the effect that this was not as he understood matters: as far as he was concerned, he had been advised by Todt and Montezemolo that his own proposed contract was one of absolute parity when it came to technical equipment and race strategy. If this was not the case, Gerhard hinted, then somebody was being economical with the truth.

'Jean Todt has assured me of equal status and materials,' he said. 'Ferrari will not change its policy of having its two drivers on the same level and status.'

Even so, despite this outwardly trenchant stance, Berger began a gentle retreat from this position when he held a press conference at Spa. His favourite option still seemed to be Ferrari, he confirmed, yet he made it clear that he would let Maranello know if and when he had finally made up his mind on the subject. He would not be hurried into a decision.

'We've both said some bad things,' he admitted, 'but we must start again with a clean sheet. If we still don't get on, we will have to be professional about it, sit down and sort it out.' In fact, on closer reflection, Berger was not so sure. He didn't want to walk away from Maranello just as the team seemed poised to become a consistent winning force. Handing Schumacher the benefit of his own efforts over the previous three seasons would be a hard pill to swallow. Eventually, however, Berger's deeply pragmatic streak asserted itself. Playing second fiddle to a driver of Schumacher's calibre was not how he envisaged the sunset of his front-line F1 career. Within another couple of weeks he signed to join Benetton with Alesi.

On reflection, he was being remarkably confident for a man who, so many people believed, had little option but to sign another two-year contract at $12 million per year with Ferrari. Not so. Gerhard's well-oiled appreciation of the dollar could not overlook other deeply serious discussions. On the day of the Belgian Grand Prix he celebrated his 36th birthday. He'd invested the past three years of his professional life with Ferrari – six, when you take into account his spell from 1987–89 – and he wasn't getting any younger.

Between 1990 and 1992 he had spent three educative years playing second fiddle to the legendary Ayrton Senna in the McLaren-Honda squad and was thus well acquainted with the implications of being partnered alongside the man popularly acclaimed as the best driver of his era. However, there were differences. He admired Senna and had come to be regarded by the ascetic Brazilian as one of his few true friends in motor racing. Frankly, Gerhard doubted whether he would ever strike up quite the same rapport with Michael Schumacher, a driver not known for his warmth or humour.

Just before Monza, Berger made his decision. He opted to go with Alesi to Benetton, which left the Ferrari management embarrassingly wrong-footed in the week leading up to the Italian Grand Prix, and stirred up a frenzy of speculation that David Coulthard would join Maranello as Schumacher's running-mate.

The Italian media went into top gear. If it wasn't going to be Coulthard, perhaps it would be Barrichello? Or Mika Salo, the young Finnish rising star at Tyrrell? Or even Italy's own Pierluigi Martini? Amazingly, the speculation seemed to focus remarkably little on the undoubted merits of Ferrari's own test driver Nicola Larini, the accomplished young man who'd stood in so ably for the injured Alesi at Imola in 1994 and come away with a strong second place behind Schumacher's Benetton-Ford.

Schumacher seemed unofficially to bless Coulthard as a possible number two, although the truth was that David by now had committed himself to the McLaren-Mercedes squad as the long-term conseqence of negotiations which took place almost 12 months earlier. Meanwhile, the *tifosi* adopted its own idiosyncratic view of the proceedings, clearly feeling that this cool, calculating German had undermined Alesi's position at Maranello. 'Better one Alesi today than 100 Schumachers tomorrow,' read a provocative banner at the paddock gates.

Coulthard further elevated himself in the eyes of the Monza fans by dominating both qualifying sessions to take pole position for Williams, with Schumacher lining up second and Berger salvaging third place on the grid, less by far than he had hoped for. Gerhard lost his first Saturday qualifying run due to an engine problem and the V12's electronic control box was changed only just in time for him to surge into contention. Alesi, meanwhile, could not better fifth place after his freshly fitted engine seemed to be delivering its power in a frustratingly inconsistent fashion.

Come the race, Coulthard blotted his copybook by spinning on the parade lap, but if Schumacher thought he was going to have a free run from his solus position on the front row, he was mistaken. A first lap collision among some of the backmarkers meant that the race was red-flagged to a halt first time round, allowing Coulthard to take his position on the grid with the spare Williams.

At the restart, the Scot took an immediate lead from Berger, with Schumacher now third ahead of Hill, a slight gap to Alesi and then Herbert's Benetton, Barrichello's Jordan and Mika Hakkinen's McLaren-Mercedes. Coulthard gradually eased away from his pursuers before spinning off at the second chicane when a front wheel bearing seized only 14 laps into the 53-lap race.

The crowd now woke up with a start. Berger's Ferrari was left leading by 1.4sec from Schumacher, with Hill right on the Benetton's tail and Alesi closing on them both. On lap 21 Schumacher was slowed slightly as he came up to lap Taki Inoue's Footwork-Hart on the outside of Curva Grande, but Hill was anxious not to lose ground as they overtook the slower car and pulled level with the Japanese driver while they braked for the second chicane.

Suddenly Schumacher seemed to be slowing more dramatically than Hill had originally anticipated. Despite going hard onto the brakes, Damon could not prevent his Williams from plunging into the back of his arch-rival's Benetton. The two cars pirouetted into the gravel trap, much to Michael's disgust, and the two men were once

As David Coulthard's Williams takes an immediate lead in Portugal, Alesi and Berger choose a narrow and a wide line respectively as they try to keep up with the Renault-propelled opposition (ICN UK Bureau).

again left to sort out their personal differences at the trackside.

The fans couldn't have cared less. Damon had done them a favour, effectively delivering a Ferrari 1-2 at the head of the field as Berger continued to surge round ahead of the pack with Alesi a few seconds behind. On lap 25, Gerhard made an over-long 17.7sec refuelling stop, delayed by a slight clutch problem, so although Jean's sister car was actually at rest for slightly longer when it came in next time round, he got away cleanly and just squeezed through ahead.

The last Ferrari 1-2 at Monza had been achieved seven years earlier when Berger and Alboreto inherited the result after Ayrton Senna's hitherto dominant McLaren-Honda had tripped over a backmarker – Jean-Louis Schlesser's Williams – only a couple of laps from the chequered flag. Now in 1995 a set of similar circumstances had given Jean a leg-up into the lead, but Ferrari's miserable run of luck had certainly not finished.

The crowd's boundless joy lasted a mere three laps. Then the on-car television camera mounted on the left-hand extremity of Alesi's rear wing broke loose, bouncing down the road behind him and slamming into the left front suspension of Berger's 412T2. The impact broke the left-hand steering arm, mercifully as Gerhard was braking for the second chicane, and the disbelieving Austrian slithered to a halt at the side of the road.

Apart from obvious relief that this wayward accessory had not made very smart contact with his helmet, Gerhard could also count himself extremely lucky that the incident had not occurred at any point on the circuit where the Ferraris were running flat out in top gear. 'This thing was coming for me at 180mph and I couldn't swerve,' he reported. 'I'm just glad it hit the car and not me.'

Alesi escaped from the incident unscathed and continued in command until eight laps from the chequered flag. Then he too began to experience trouble with his car. Over the radio to the pits, he explained that he thought he had picked up a puncture in one of the rear tyres. 'The car began to feel as though it was on three wheels,' he later recounted, 'but it wasn't a puncture, it was a wheel bearing failure.'

By the time Alesi was mid-way round his 46th lap, flames were licking round the Ferrari's rear suspension, the car slowed suddenly and Jean aimed it for the pit lane. Unfastening his belts, he climbed out and walked over to the pit wall where he slumped down, head in hands, utterly desolate. Silently, the grandstands began to empty as Johnny Herbert pressed on to inherit another lucky win for Benetton.

'Nobody could blame the drivers for what happened at Monza,' said John Barnard, 'although I'm bound to wonder how Alesi could have covered over 2500km there in testing and have no problems.' Play back the video of the 1995 Italian GP and you'll get a strong feel for the implication behind that remark. Alesi seemed to spend far too much time man-handling his Ferrari over the brutally disruptive kerbs during his spell at the front of the field.

In the wake of this crushing disappointment, one could detect that the whole Ferrari effort was beginning to unravel. In such cases, when a team is facing a wholesale re-organisation for the following year, this is not unusual. The process starts almost imperceptibly, but eventually gains an obvious momentum. The drivers begin to lose the fine edge of their motivation, and technical development on the cars eases up as the effort switches towards finalising the development of a new machine for next year.

Barnard made no bones about it. 'I suppose the bottom line was that we died a bit on the aerodynamic side mid-season. We under-estimated certain factors and, although we had what we regarded as fundamentally a good car, and were pushing hard on development, we didn't really find anything new.

'For Silverstone we had started to look at revised quarter panels for the rear bodywork, fiddling with changes to the Coke panels (the waisted rear deck section curving inside the rear wheels) and we also had a new front wing package which we tried for the first time at Spa, in addition to changing the rear suspension geometry a few times.

'In general, taking the season as a whole, what surprised us most was that we began developing higher downforce loadings on the wheels than we had seen before, even though the new rules were primarily intended to reduce downforce.'

Technical development on the cars continued for the Portuguese GP at Estoril where both 412T2s appeared during the Friday morning free practice sessions with revised nose sections incorporating new front wings designed to offer enhanced downforce with no significant extra drag. However, by the time the cars appeared in first qualifying they had reverted to their earlier Monza-spec configuration.

Gerhard had some fun on the first afternoon, apparently chopping across Schumacher's Benetton at the moment Ferrari's new recruit was making a bid for fastest time. Michael was extremely frosty about the whole affair, expressing himself 'a bit angry with my friend Gerhard who messed up a very good lap of mine. When you are on the track the idea is that you always take care of other drivers, but on this occasion he didn't do it, so I am a little disappointed.'

With the innocent insouciance he affects so well, Berger replied: 'I must apologise to Schumacher for having blocked him. I had not seen him and suddenly in a corner he was right behind me when I was on my warm-up lap. I don't think it really caused him much of a problem as I started my quick lap immediately after the incident.'

Gerhard duly qualified fourth behind Coulthard, Hill and Schumacher, but Alesi

Time for a change. Eddie Jordan (left) shakes hands with Jean Todt after cementing the deal which saw Eddie Irvine released from his contract to join Ferrari alongside Michael Schumacher in 1996 (ICN UK Bureau).

somehow got lost on chassis set-up and slipped back to seventh in the final order. As at Monza, the race was initially red-flagged to a halt after Ukyo Katayama's Tyrrell and Pedro Lamy's Minardi were involved in a spectacular collision which totally blocked the circuit.

Come the restart, Coulthard accelerated cleanly away from pole position into an immediate lead and went on to dominate the race, winning easily while Hill and Schumacher battled over second place. Meanwhile, in the Ferrari camp, the race was destined to end with much bad feeling after Berger and Alesi finished fourth and fifth. Alesi erupted from the cockpit, accusing Jean Todt of having deliberately favoured Gerhard in terms of race strategy, couching his criticism in particularly trenchant terms when confronted by the Italian television cameras. It seemed as if this was the final blow to scupper Alesi's relationship with Maranello once and for all.

The difficulty arose because both men were adhering to different fuel stop strategies, Jean deciding to stop only twice while Gerhard opted for three stops. Alesi was furious when Gerhard, running quicker on fresh rubber after his second stop on lap 33, came up behind him and Todt asked him to give way. Alesi declined the invitation, so Gerhard was brought in 11 laps ahead of schedule for his final stop on lap 45 and eventually squeezed ahead of Jean when the Frenchman made his own second stop two laps later.

'Todt has been a problem for me all year and he has broken my balls,' seethed the enraged Alesi. 'If it has to be like this, I would rather not bother.' When Ferrari fined him $200,000 he told Berger it was good value for money. Todt, however, remained diplomatically soothing in response: 'Jean has a generous nature, but an emotional temperament. We have given him maximum support for five seasons and will continue to do so for the last four races of the season.'

Before the next race, the European GP at Nurburgring, Ferrari finally announced the identity of Schumacher's team-mate for 1996. That fortunate individual would be Eddie Irvine, the outspoken and rather bluff Ulsterman who by now had run out of patience with the Jordan-Peugeot team's progress. Jean Todt explained why he believed that F1's most high-profile maverick – whose 1993 dust-up with Senna further enhanced his reputation as an iconoclast – was ultimately deemed the right man for the job:

'We needed a very talented driver to make a strong team with Michael Schumacher. I think that everybody knows that I have a very good friendship with Eddie Jordan. I told him frankly that Ferrari was interested. We knew that Eddie (Irvine) had discussed the possibility of getting out of his Jordan contract, I talked about it with Eddie Jordan and finally we made the deal.

'Of course I informed Michael about the possibility of Irvine. He was very happy about it because he knows that it could be a good pairing. We don't want to rely only on one driver to win races. We want to work for both the Drivers' and the Constructors' Championships, so it was important to have a second driver who could win races. We really wanted to have a very good team for next year.

'I said before that it is important to have things clear from the beginning. As World Champion, Michael is number one in the team. Eddie is number two.' Gerhard

Berger's concern on this matter had clearly been well justified.

Nevertheless, Todt was quick to insist that Ferrari would be working to field two equal cars in 1996. 'Next year we will have two top drivers, as we did this year,' he explained, 'and if we want them to win we have to give them the best car. We cannot expect them to win if we don't. So, firstly, it is up to us to give them a competitive car.

'Michael is not making demands about the T-car. I remind you that Ferrari is employing Michael Schumacher, it is not Michael Schumacher who is employing Ferrari. Of course, we are very happy to have him – he is a great guy. He is 26 years old, but when you have a discussion with him, you find a guy who thinks, who speaks,

Pressuring the tyres. One of the many detailed jobs so easily taken for granted by the casual F1 observer (LAT).

who understands, in a fantastic way. I have not met many people like him. But he is going to drive for a team.'

So was Ferrari's decision to employ the care-free, outspoken Irvine a gesture to Michael that Todt is in charge of the team?

'I spoke with Eddie very clearly,' he replied. 'He has a strong personality, but we need somebody with a strong personality if we want to help the team, improve it and get results. Otherwise we would have entered just one car.

'So we want to have two top guys, and to have somebody who is really happy to be with Michael. We also want Michael to be happy to be with Eddie. So, before the wedding, everything is nice and everything is beautiful. But sometimes things change when you are really living together. So sometimes we will have hard days, but I'm used to that.'

Ferrari's decision to buy Irvine from Jordan had been finalised only a week after the British team confirmed that Eddie would stay in the driver line-up alongside Barrichello for 1996. What was not immediately obvious from the touchlines was that Irvine had wanted out from his Jordan deal, almost at any price. He felt that the team's progress had been lagging disappointingly, so Eddie Jordan was quite willing to activate Irvine's buy-out clause and let him go, reputedly for a figure in the region of $5 million.

'Never in its existence since 1982 has Jordan ever deliberately deprived or hindered a young driver under contract from advancing his career,' said Jordan in a tone of lofty altruism. 'If Eddie Irvine got the chance to go to Ferrari, I'm sure we would have come to the right conclusion. That is not to say we are softies. This team is bigger than any man. But you cannot hold back a young boy like Eddie Irvine when he is offered an opportunity like Ferrari.'

For his part, Irvine said all the right things too: 'Jordan was the team which brought me into F1 and I have had a good two years there. The start was bad, but it got better and I felt more comfortable as time went on. It was one of the best teams with which to come into F1 because the pressure on me was not too high. We have progressed although we've had bad reliability this year. I believe that Jordan is going to be very strong next year, but not as good as Ferrari.

'To me, this is the ultimate challenge. Michael is for sure the best driver in F1, and for me the whole point about being in F1 is to be measured against the best. I now have the perfect opportunity.'

What Irvine failed to mention was his first meeting with Montezemolo. He had button-holed the Ferrari President in the paddock at Buenos Aires, first asking if he was who he thought he was and, once satisfied with his identity, making a plea for a discount on spare parts for his 1982 Ferrari GTO. Luca didn't quite know how to react, but the Ulsterman's cheerful open approach struck a chord with the Ferrari boss and he mentally kept an eye on Eddie's progress from that point onward.

As if fired by this high-profile promotion, Irvine qualified the Jordan fifth at Nurburgring, splitting Berger and Alesi in the starting line-up. Both Ferraris featured revised side pods for this, the final race of the European season, and both men reported they offered a slight, but perceptible, improvement. Alesi's problems at Estoril clearly seemed to have been put behind him and he seemed in a sunny mood all weekend.

Come race day, however, it was the dismal weather which preoccupied everybody's thoughts. Low cloud and drenching rain generated a mood of apprehension, foreboding even. By the time the cars trickled out on their parade laps, the track was showing signs of drying out on the racing line. But it was still bitterly cold and the question of how long tyre temperatures would take to come up became another crucial factor in the tactical equation.

Most front-runners opted for deep-grooved rain tyres, but Ferrari took a major gamble on the starting grid. Off came the rain tyres on both 412T2s, up went the ride heights, and both Alesi and Berger set off on their parade laps running on slicks.

Coulthard, who'd repeated his Monza faux pas by spinning off on his out-lap before

Gerhard Berger, feeling the tension rise as the start approaches (LAT).

144

even getting to the grid, again found himself starting from pole in the spare Williams FW17B but still managed to open out a slight lead in the first few laps. Hill was second at the end of the opening lap ahead of Berger, Irvine and Alesi and, within half-a-dozen laps, it became clear that the rain was holding off and the track was definitely drying out.

On lap 11, Schumacher and Hill came in for slicks, followed a lap later by Coulthard, allowing Alesi to surge past into the lead. By lap 20 the Ferrari was in a class of its own, 28sec ahead of Coulthard. By lap 24 Jean had opened the advantage to 43.5sec, and it was by now clear that he was settling on a one-stop strategy.

On lap 34 – half distance – Alesi brought his scarlet challenger in for a 15.8sec stop and resumed, set on a non-stop run to the flag, with 4.6sec in hand over Hill's Williams. Damon was well wound up by this stage and quickly closed in for the kill, only to find Alesi downright disobliging when he attempted to overtake on lap 40, the Williams-Renault losing its nose section against the Ferrari's left rear tyre.

Hill would recover to pull up to fourth in the closing stages before crashing heavily. That left Schumacher to come surging up onto Alesi's tail, nipping ahead of the Ferrari with only three laps left to run. Many observers concluded that Jean had simply gone to sleep, but in reality the V12 was strapped for fuel and Alesi was forced to back off to avoid running out before the finish. It was a Montreal scenario all over again. He was just over two seconds behind the Benetton as they passed the chequered flag.

'My strategy was the right one for the conditions,' reflected Alesi after the race. 'I really gave my all and the only thing I am unhappy about is that I had difficulty getting

Todt and Alesi reviewing their last season together (LAT).

past some of the backmarkers in the final stages of the race. This prevented me from maintaining my pace; there is a new rule about overtaking, but the marshals did not do the right thing with the blue flags. I don't know what to say about my crash with Hill. Suddenly I felt a bump, but Damon did it all by himself.'

While attempting to lap Mika Hakkinen's McLaren, Jean had gone straight on at the chicane, a detour which cost him seven seconds of his lead over Schumacher, allowing Michael to close to within three seconds of his Ferrari. 'My tyres had gone off, especially at the front and I could not fight off Schumacher,' he continued. 'His move was completely correct, and if we touched a little, it was just because there was nowhere else for the wheels to go!'

Gerhard, meanwhile, had another miserable race. From the start he was left grappling with a handling imbalance, probably caused by an incorrectly pressured set of tyres, and he stopped for good after 40 laps while running fourth. His problem was yet another failure of the crank sensor, a malfunction which had blighted his efforts all too frequently during the course of the season.

'On my second set of tyres the car was much better, but suddenly my engine started to misfire, as had already happened at Spa,' he shrugged. 'When I made my second stop, the engine died and would not restart.'

As an aside, the European GP also marked the end of a spell of uncertainty surrounding Niki Lauda's position as a consultant to the Ferrari F1 team. Over the previous few months, Niki had made some personal observations to the press about certain aspects of the team's progress which were interpreted in some quarters as the official company line.

This wasn't necessarily the case, but Todt was obviously irked by the situation. It seemed as though Lauda was being regarded as some kind of informal team manager. It was briefly mooted that the former triple champion would be transferred to some sort of globe-trotting PR role for the road car division, but Montezemolo eventually reaffirmed his confidence in his old colleague and Niki stayed on as before.

The 1995 season ended with an intensive rush of activity. The Pacific GP had originally been scheduled to take place earlier in the season at Japan's TI Circuit, but the Kobe earthquake so disrupted communications in the area that the event was postponed. After much negotiation and debate, it was eventually re-scheduled just one week before the Japanese GP would take place at the Suzuka track near Nagoya. It was a logistical nightmare. The teams bridled with indignation at this frenzy of racing, a situation further aggravated by the fact that the season's finale, the Australian GP at Adelaide, was only a fortnight after Suzuka.

By now, the Ferraris were falling away quite perceptibly from the front-running pace. Alesi and Berger arrived in Japan suffering from, respectively, 'flu and jet lag, and could only qualify fourth and fifth. Coulthard qualified on pole from Hill with Schumacher third on the inside of the second row.

This was Hill's final opportunity to keep the championship battle alive, although such a forlorn mathematical outside chance as to be scarcely worth thinking about. Nevertheless, he made a robust getaway in second place behind his Williams team-mate as the pack sprinted to the first tricky, medium-speed right-hander at the end of the start/finish straight.

When the fast-starting Schumacher attempted to go round the outside of Hill, Damon stuck to his line, sliding ever so slightly wide to push the Benetton up the kerb and allow Alesi to nip past into second place. Jean was thus able to finish the opening lap 2.7sec behind Coulthard, in second place ahead of Hill, Berger and Schumacher. While Jean held up Hill sufficiently for Coulthard to make good his escape, Schumacher elbowed his way ahead of Gerhard on the fourth lap and quickly closed on Hill. But on this occasion Damon was having none of it, driving with a defensive elan which angered Michael considerably.

At the end of lap 19, Alesi, Hill and Schumacher came hurtling into the pits in nose-to-tail formation – second, third and fourth – for their first refuelling stop. They resumed with Schumacher second, Alesi briefly fourth behind Irvine's Jordan and Hill back to sixth. Five laps later, Jean dived inside the future Ferrari man at the end of the back straight, but Hill displayed his magnetic attraction for rival machinery and bumped the Jordan as he made to go through, fortunately without damage to either car.

At the end of the day, Schumacher capitalised again on Benetton's refuelling wizardry to trounce both Coulthard and Hill. Berger and Alesi wound up fourth and fifth, lapped by the Renault-engined trio. 'Nothing much to say,' nodded Gerhard. 'The car felt fine, nicely balanced. We just didn't have enough grip.' More crucially for Maranello, Schumacher had clinched his second World Championship and would be bringing the coveted race number one to Ferrari in 1996 for the first time since Jody Scheckter some 16 years before.

A week later at Suzuka, both Williams drivers grappled with set-up problems during qualifying and it was Alesi who carried the battle to Schumacher, qualifying his Ferrari a brilliant second only 0.8sec away from the pole position Benetton. Berger was fifth, splitting Hill and Coulthard, while Mika Hakkinen's McLaren-Mercedes was a new interloper to be reckoned with in third place on the grid.

The weather conditions on race day seemed potentially as treacherously unpredictable as they had been at Nurburgring. The track surface was still wet by the time the field accelerated away on the parade lap, but the heavy rain had eased and it would obviously not take too long for the drivers to be requiring a switch from rain tyres to slicks.

Schumacher just got the jump on Alesi, Hakkinen and Hill, completing the opening lap with Hakkinen, Hill, Irvine, Coulthard and Berger leading the pursuit. Then came disaster. On lap four, the Ferrari pit was informed that *both* its drivers had incurred a 10sec stop-go penalty for jumping the start.

Alesi came in next time round to take his medicine, dropping from second to tenth, while Gerhard was in on lap six, losing nine places. On lap seven, Alesi came slamming round the flat-out left-hander before the pits, overtook Herbert's Benetton, and then cut right across in front of the Englishman in order to come in for a switch to slicks. It was a characteristically nerve-jangling performance but, as it turned out, calculated to bring out the best in him on this particular occasion.

Stopping so soon for slicks proved a master stroke for Alesi, providing him with an enormous advantage on a track surface which was now drying out fast. He dropped from tenth to 15th, but as his rivals all came in for their own tyre changes, he came storming back through the field in meteoric fashion, hardly losing any time at all when Lamy's Minardi edged him into a high speed 360-degree spin on the grass opposite the pits.

After Hill's first refuelling stop, he resumed just ahead of Jean, but the flying Ferrari forced its way through to get ahead of the Williams on lap 10. By the time that first flurry of refuelling stops had taken place, the order settled down with Alesi now back into second place and closing on Schumacher. By lap 19 he got to within a second of the leading Benetton – but that's as close as he was allowed. Six laps later he rolled to a halt out on the circuit.

Initially it was concluded that the differential had failed, but closer scrutiny revealed that a driveshaft joint inside the gearbox had broken. Had it been caused by that wild spin down the grass as he avoided Lamy? Perhaps, but there was no way anybody could pinpoint this as the definite reason. Either way, it was another depressing retirement for Ferrari, doubly disappointing as Berger had suffered yet another crank sensor failure and pulled off after 16 laps while running ninth.

'It would be presumptuous of me to say I could have won,' reflected Alesi. 'However, I would certainly have fought for it all the way to the end. The thing I wanted most this season was to win at Monza. Things went badly there, but the desire to win once more before leaving Ferrari is still there. I tried again today, but I was in a bad mood, as I was convinced I did not jump the start. The grid slopes downhill and I only have two feet; one for the accelerator and one for the clutch. If the car moved forward by a few centimetres it was certainly not intentional. I will try once more to win in Australia in two weeks' time.'

Berger, meanwhile, was barely able to conceal his annoyance. 'This was the same sensor that has given me problems in other races,' he shrugged. 'I don't know what to say. As for my penalty, I really think the control system (on the grid) is not very good. I realised that the car had started to move forward as the track slopes downhill, and so I braked. Because of that I made a bad start and dropped two places. And they describe that as a jumped start!'

From here on in, it was simply a question of getting the season finished. Schumacher was anxious to sample a Ferrari, while both Alesi and Berger were keen to get a taste of Renault V10 power with the Benetton B196. The Australian GP at Adelaide just might have provided a fairy-tale ending to the Ferrari careers of either driver – but didn't. A joint total of 11 years' endeavour for the Prancing Horse ended in ignominy yet again.

Gerhard lasted until lap 31 when, running second, his V12 exploded in a cloud of oil, smoke and spume. Alesi had been eliminated eight laps earlier while battling for second with Schumacher. Unaccountably, he'd turned into the Benetton's left rear wheel at the end of the back straight and the two cars collided. Michael survived a few more laps before stopping with damaged suspension, while Jean came straight in to retire almost immediately.

Schumacher was thus deprived of a chance to score a record tenth win in a single season, although in fairness it looked as though second place behind Hill's dominant Williams was the best he could hope for on this particular occasion. That didn't prevent him from being extremely annoyed, however:

'It was a very unnecessary action that Alesi took, because I was clearly faster than him. I don't understand what was going on in his brain. Was it switched off? He'd better keep out of my way at the Benetton party tonight, because this wasn't the way I wanted to finish the season. OK, the Williams was quicker, but I would have been happy to finish second here today.' Alesi offered no explanation.

An end-of-season assessment proved disappointing. Ferrari (73 points) had finished third in the Constructors' Championship, but it was a distant third behind Benetton (137 points) and Williams (112 points). The team had won a single victory and, whichever way it was sliced, had been short on engine performance and mechanical reliability. Ferraris failed to finish races 15 times this season.

In the background, Jean Todt quietly voiced his caution about the team's prospects for 1996. A logical and calm individual, Todt had always worked hard to separate his ability for detailed, rational analysis from the euphoria of the moment. In his view, the driver changes were only part of a much wider and more complex picture.

'Michael Schumacher is the best driver, no doubt, but this guy needs a very good car,' said Todt at Suzuka. 'We must not expect that we will solve all our problems by having

Michael driving for us. This would be a big mistake. It will help, obviously, and will be a big motivating factor for the team. But I know we have to work hard to give him the best support – better support, in fact, than we have been able to offer our present drivers.'

Ferrari's Sporting Director did not mince his words when expressing his disappointment at the team's 1995 performance: 'We cannot always try to find excuses. We must produce results. The 1994 season was much better than the year before, but this year we had been expecting about 20 per cent further progress. As things turned out, I estimate we have made about 10 per cent progress, so we are effectively 10 per cent behind target. In addition, next year we also have a new V10 engine which raises concern about reliability and quality control problems.'

John Barnard summed up the fortunes of one of the best looking Grand Prix cars of its era: 'We did have reliability problems. Engine problems, some chassis problems, administrative problems and some driver-inflicted problems. Certainly, I do think that for the first part of the season it was potentially the best car out there; certainly equal to the Williams as far as Monaco.

'Think about it. Jean was a close second at Buenos Aires, Gerhard a possible winner at Imola if he hadn't stalled at a refuelling stop, and at Monaco Jean could have made a race of it if he hadn't had the disastrous second qualifying and been on the front row.

'That said, having seen Schumacher perform in the first couple of winter test sessions with us, I know we would have had to have the best car out there by some measure in order to beat the guy!'

Barnard is not an easy man to impress, but he was certainly very taken with Schumacher – with his analytical cool, his maturity for a young man in his mid-twenties. And his sheer speed. 'People like Schumacher are a step up, they are on another level. There are good guys out there, like Alesi and Berger. But then you've got the special ones – Senna, Prost, I suppose Lauda and, going back, the likes of Clark and Stewart.

'They are just bloody quick. There's no major philosophy about it. They're quick. He's very mature for his age and has a great deal of inbuilt confidence. He goes out there and puts in some consistently quick times. He's obviously driving at that speed without strain, without thinking about going quickly, because when he comes back he has a load of information in his head about all the corners around the track.

'That's all we want him to do. We don't want him to engineer, just relate to us what the car is doing all the way through all the corners – going in, middle of the corner, coming out. And he's clear-cut. And he has a great feel for changing conditions. There's no panic. If you've got tyres that are going off, he doesn't get excited in the "oh shit, where have we lost half a second?" style. It's just "I think it's time for a fresh set of tyres". It's all under control, never looking for fictitious excuses.'

He was interested to note that Schumacher had his own individualistic oversteering set-up. 'He wants the nose to turn in at any time and he's prepared to dial the back end in and out, a high wire act, by working the throttle. But if he's turning the lap times, that's fine!'

For Barnard, Schumacher's technique represented a fascinating contrast to the style adopted by Alain Prost in the heyday of the McLaren-TAG turbos. 'Alain would drive a car that other drivers would complain would understeer off the track,' he recalled.

'But the way he drove it made it work. I think a lot of his style came from driving turbo cars when the trick was not to go into the corners too quickly, but really get onto the throttle early because of the turbo lag. By the time the engine sorted itself out you were already halfway round the corner and that's when you want the power. Also, with the turbo cars, when the power came in, it came in with a rush, so you had to get as

Ferrari's most able test driver for the past few seasons has been Nicola Larini and many observers were surprised when Eddie Irvine beat him to the second seat alongside Schumacher for 1996 (LAT).

much aero download as possible on the back of the car to get it to stick and cope with all this power rush.

'The front end was very lightly loaded aerodynamically, which meant you had to go mechanically soft to get the grip and turn in. But in order to do that, you couldn't just barrel into the corner and jerk the wheel a la Mansell and Rosberg, if you like.'

Barnard also made the obvious point that it is a treat for any chief designer to work with a driver of Schumacher's calibre. 'Obviously, it's satisfying because he's most likely to get the maximum potential out of your car. You're never really sure with the other guys. When he (Schumacher) is driving another car, it really needles you, because you're not certain whether the opposition has got a better car than yours. Or whether it's him!'

The long-awaited type 044 3-litre V10 was assessed by Schumacher at Fiorano only five days after he'd retired from the Australian GP in Adelaide. Installed in a revised

412T2 chassis, this was a test hack designed simply to get the engine running out on the circuit, rather than a finely-tuned machine in which Schumacher could post realistic, comparative times in the first off-season test at Estoril during late November.

Interestingly, for comparison purposes Michael was also given a lot of running in the existing V12-engined car. It was an exercise which provided a graphic illustration of just what a talent Ferrari had now invested in. Without too much fuss, Schumacher posted a 1min 21.21sec lap at Estoril, 0.7sec faster than Berger's fourth place qualifying time for the 1995 Portuguese GP and 0.1sec inside his own best time in the Benetton-Renault B196.

Winter testing at Estoril has become something of a ritual. The Portuguese track is employed as an off-season venue as the weather tends to be reasonably temperate. Even with a stiff wind blowing in off the Atlantic, more worthwhile feedback can be achieved here than at a frosty December Silverstone where tyres refuse to build up any decent working temperature and mechanics are chilled to the bone.

Yet team engineers are always quick to point out that off-season testing proves nothing. Nobody knows how much fuel each individual car is carrying, therefore its overall weight is in doubt. Designers pooh-pooh any comparisons so drawn. But Estoril testing is inevitably a narcotic affair. Engineers and journalists, together with those drivers not yet involved, swap anecdote and speculation almost daily.

On this occasion, the cross-referencing process took on a nice edge with Alesi and Berger also having their first taste of the Benetton so recently vacated by Schumacher. Michael quickly came to grips with the Italian V12 and generally confirmed the pleasure in its handling characteristic originally expressed by Jean and Gerhard.

'I was pleasantly surprised how quickly it all came together,' said the German. 'The car was obviously more stable than the Benetton on the limit and it felt better in fast corners. It is also the best racing car I have even driven in the wet!'

He enthused on what he described as the V12 engine's seamless power delivery: 'as good as a Renault in every way'. This was a touch of psychological warfare, one suspects. At a stroke, he was attempting to unsettle Alesi and Berger by floating the idea that they really should have won more races in 1995, while at the same time displaying his own prowess.

The new V10 was less obviously outstanding on its first serious test run. Three development units were to hand, but one lost power on the first day. The second suffered a camshaft breakage, the third sprang an oil leak. In addition, there were failures of the engine mounting plates where they picked up on the 412T2 chassis. Much work needed to be done on this front, at least.

Irvine, meanwhile, was kept very much in the background until just before Christmas 1995 when he was allowed his first serious run in the V10-engined V12 chassis at Estoril. Some people find the Ulsterman a little too laid back for their taste, but there was no doubting that he had a passionate enthusiasm for Ferrari, even if he kept his feelings in a very clear perspective as he recounted to Maurice Hamilton in *Autosport*.

'People used to talk about the mystique surrounding Ferrari and Maranello and all that,' he said. 'But you have to say that Maranello is not a pretty sight! I've always liked the road cars, but when you see so many in one place, the whole thing loses something. But if you see just one parked in your local high street, Wow! I used to get on my bike and ride for miles just to look at a Ferrari.

'It's all relative. I can remember racing at Kirkistown and places like that and talking about people like Mauricio Gugelmin. "What a mega! He's a Formula 3 driver!" Even so, I have to admit that the reception from the *tifosi* was just stunning. On the day of the launch at Maranello, they were lining the route between Fiorano and the place

Luca di Montezemolo pondering a future in which Ferrari could once again scale the Big Time (LAT).

where we had the press conference. The reception along the way was pretty special.'

That said, his first outing at Estoril left Schumacher's quality as the team's number one driver very firmly imprinted on Irvine's psyche. 'During the first few days of our first test at Estoril, Michael was finding half a second through the two quick corners. But in the slow stuff, it swung back and forth between us.

'We were very similar – which was good, because it's been said that he has the time in the slow stuff. He was blindingly quick in the fast corners and that was to be expected because he had already done five days with the Ferrari at Estoril. I had just arrived, was finding my way and hadn't built up confidence.

'I didn't have the right set-up to start with, which was interesting, because Michael, who had started out the same way, had experienced the same problems I had. So on set-up, we seem to be very similar, which is good.

'Our driving styles also seem to be much the same. I turn in very gently, which is what he does. It doesn't make sense to turn the wheel sharp, left or right, which is what a lot of drivers do. Anyone who has tried a car the way I like it set up has usually said it had too much oversteer which, when I think back on it, is perhaps a good thing because it means that they were turning in too quickly.

'Michael's team-mates have tended to say the same thing. OK, he may take another step forwards, but we seem to think along the same lines.'

Chapter Seven

Limbering up for the Championship

If there was a crucial date to be singled out in recent Ferrari F1 history, it would have to be Thursday, 15 February 1996. In watery winter sunshine, the new Ferrari F310 was rolled out for its official unveiling on the tarmac at the team's Fiorano test track.

Standing alongside the new machine, immaculately spiffed up in their new red overalls, were Michael Schumacher, Eddie Irvine and Ferrari's highly experienced F1 test driver Nicola Larini. Ferrari President Luca di Montezemolo was present, together with the Director of Research and Development, John Barnard and, in what was regarded in some quarters as a gesture of divine blessing, Fiat overlord Gianni Agnelli arrived in a clattering helicopter. The Dream Team was seemingly complete.

By popular acclaim, the new Ferrari was a gorgeous-looking machine. At first glance, it seemed like a logical evolution of the previous season's design concept, but on closer examination it proved to be very different. It was also late, the last of the 1996 breed of F1 cars to break cover, which meant that opportunities for testing prior to the first race of the season, in Melbourne on 10 March, were distinctly limited.

The F310 profile reflected more than 10 months' intensive wind tunnel development work by John Barnard at the British Aerospace Filton facility. Barnard described the car as 'semi-high nose' but would not be drawn into a detailed discussion of its under-chassis aerodynamics. Most distinctively, the sidepods resembled the elongated oval ducts used on the dismal Ferrari F92A back in 1992, a car on which Barnard had precious little technical input. Those sidepod inlets are separated from the monocoque edge by distinct 'shoulders' and the car featured a pronounced aerodynamic 'splitter' under the cockpit designed to duct the air into the radiators.

Barnard was quick to point out that only the leading section of the car's underside featured an aerodynamic 'double floor' which stops and exits immediately ahead of the radiator. 'I wasn't around here in 1992, of course, and the radiator thing was not the key problem with the F92A. When I came back to Ferrari I looked with interest at that project. Taking the undercut sidepod all the way back would require the radiator to be pushed up, sacrificing centre of gravity considerations.'

As far as the suspension was concerned, the new Ferrari retained torsion bar suspension front and rear but a totally new transverse six-speed gearbox was employed to capitalise on the car's revised aerodynamic package.

So what about the engine? The F310's power came from an all-new 75-degree, 2998.1cc V10 featuring four pneumatically-activated valves per cylinder and variable

Michael Schumacher with the F310 at Paul Ricard, pre-season testing, 1996. First signs are that the new car was not quite powerful enough (Darren Heath).

Schumacher makes a firm point to former Honda engineer Osamu Goto (Darren Heath).

inlet trumpets. It was the work of Paolo Martinelli's engine department with key input from former Honda F1 engineer Osamu Goto. Claims for rev limits and power outputs were vague, with general remarks of 'more than 600bhp at around 16,000rpm'. Either the Maranello crew was keeping mum or the engine needed much more development. Nobody was giving much away on this front.

Although Montezemolo played host at this gathering, it was Agnelli who set the emotional agenda, recalling his personal relationship with the late Enzo Ferrari. It was Agnelli, of course, who had masterminded Fiat's rescue of the near-bankrupt Ferrari empire back in 1969, when Enzo had come to him for help and effectively admitted that the empire was bust. He, more than anybody, understood precisely the role played by the Prancing Horse in the whole psyche of the Italian nation.

'In the 1970s we won maybe four or five World Championships together,' recalled the silver-haired Fiat chief. 'When I think about Ferrari, it is as a fan. And the fans have shown great patience over many years. Now it is time to repay them. We have the means to win the championship. We have the men. We have the best drivers on the market. Last year we had two excellent drivers in Jean Alesi and Gerhard Berger. But this year, we have something more. We have a star. All that is missing is the championship.'

Schumacher looked not the least bit embarrassed in the face of such lavish praise. However, what he did make clear was that he did not have such an in-depth feel for the traditions or atmosphere at Maranello. This, he hinted, was more due to youthful ignorance than any lack of sensitivity.

'When I started to race in cars, I did not know anything about F1 or Ferrari,' he explained with an almost compelling innocence. 'I'd arrived in motor racing very quickly, but ever since I was young I knew that Ferrari is a big part of F1, even if I did not understand why. And I am sure I will appreciate the situation more and more in the coming years.'

Needless to say, the double World Champion denied that he had come to Ferrari simply for the money, hinting that he had received one bid that was even better than the $20 million reputedly on offer from Maranello. F1 insiders believe that it was the rival Marlboro-backed McLaren-Mercedes team which pitched in with the higher sum. Clearly, even the ascetic Schumacher had been fascinated by the intangible Maranello magic.

'I have been racing since I was four years old in karts,' he explained. 'I started to race for fun, and I still enjoy myself a lot. Money is a strong component, but it is not the most important one. I have not come to Ferrari only for this, because I had another offer which was better.'

Regarding predictions about the forthcoming season, Schumacher counselled caution.

'After having seen the new car, I am much more optimistic than before. But we must be realistic. We have had a lot of problems to solve at Ferrari and you cannot solve them all in three months. It would be fantastic to win a couple of races, but I must consider that last year a Ferrari retired 13 times. Even this year I am not sure we will finish all the races. We want to be reliable in 1996, but we must go with small steps.

'I am quite comfortable inside Ferrari, but if something goes well or badly, the faults in a marriage are always half and half. For example, I am responsible for a spin, but sometimes you spin because of the car, and it is up to me to create a situation in which the technical people are able to correct the mistakes.'

There was no concealing the air of expectancy surrounding the launch of the new Ferrari F310. Upbeat optimism is the oxygen of the team's very existence at such times of the year. If Formula 1 is a complex jigsaw, then it is also very much a two-part affair. The first task on the road to success is to locate all the pieces; the second, to assemble the complete picture.

So what if Ferrari was not in a position to win in 1997, let alone 1996? Montezemolo, momentarily, seemed to prevaricate. 'This year is our final leap. Our goal is to win more races than in the past three years and to get close, by 1997, to being in a position to win the World Championship.'

Only to get close? Cynics would say that $20 million was a high price to pay for winning more than one race a year – and it certainly wasn't quite how Luca had spelled it out in Buenos Aires, almost a year earlier. He had hoped to win the World Championship in 1997, at the latest. So was Ferrari drinking at the Last Chance Saloon? Agnelli offered some solace, but only up to a point. 'First, I have never set deadlines,' he said. 'I have learned from Italian politics that a deadline is never really final.'

However, he did add in an aside to Montezemolo: 'If you don't win with this, what *do* you want?'

The new Ferrari F310 underwent its initial shakedown runs at Fiorano where slight cracks in the gearbox bellhousing, and a resultant oil leak, were detected. This problem was seemingly rectified in time for Michael Schumacher to continue the new machine's pre-season preparations at Estoril just over a fortnight before the first round of the 1996 World Championship, the Australian Grand Prix at Melbourne's lavishly remodelled Albert Park circuit.

John Barnard had originally been scheduled to make the trip to Australia with his new baby, but the British engineer eventually found it easy to resist the temptation of a 48-hour round trip cooped up in the first class cabin of a 747 and preferred to spend a week at Maranello.

While the new car was competing in its maiden race, he would spend some time evaluating the aerodynamic results from the wind tunnel at Ferrari's HQ – the UK-based tunnel at Filton was temporarily out of action in order to facilitate the completion of upgrading work. John was thus well away from the controversy which bubbled up in Australia concerning the interpretation, by two rival teams, of new technical regulations concerning lateral cockpit protection.

The bottom line was that Williams and Jordan found themselves accused, albeit obliquely, of cutting corners on safety with their interpretation of these new rules which allowed a better airflow over the rear of their machines than their rivals, including the new Ferraris. However, the FIA concluded that if Williams and Jordan could muster the technical ingenuity to interpret these rules in such an advantageous manner, then their rivals were presumably equipped to do the same. Any objections were curtly dismissed and the cars duly pronounced as totally conforming with the rules.

The Ferrari F310 was also troubled by the position of the drivers' heads interfering with the ram effect into the engine airbox, reducing power output by an estimated 10bhp and compromising the car's straightline speed.

In addition to this, both Schumacher and Irvine reported that the new car seemed aerodynamically sensitive, locking wheels under hard braking. Even so, at Melbourne Maranello's new chargers lined up third and fourth behind the Williams-Renaults of F1 new boy Jacques Villeneuve and his team-mate Damon Hill. As it turned out, Eddie just slipped in a quicker time than Michael after the World Champion was obliged to qualify his spare car because his race chassis developed gearbox trouble.

Despite this encouraging performance, Schumacher declined to revise his pre-season assessment of the team's potential. 'The situation is that we have had no testing in terms of development,' he explained. 'We were able to do a little bit of work to sort out the worst problems, but there are still little things which you have got to change, adapt, and make reliable. Whether we are going to find a lot more of these I don't know. We are pretty much on schedule, and I really want to take the first two or three races more as testing [sessions] rather than go for race results.

'We are not in a position now to think about good results and finishing races. We haven't done a proper race simulation with the new car, so it would probably be a bit of a surprise if everything goes in the normal way. But that's exactly the thing I expected when I came to Ferrari. I am pleased about the principal situation. The base is all right. There are a lot of areas potentially we can build on. I predicted that the gap to the front teams was going to be around a second – which it is, right now.'

In fact, Villeneuve's pole time was 1m 32.371s with Hill a fraction behind on 1m 32.509s. Irvine managed 1m 32.889s and Schuey 1m 33.125s. By the end of the race there would be many who were tempted to conclude that Michael was erring on the side of caution in his assessment of the task ahead.

In what was to become a highly dramatic season, the first race opened with a bang, and a re-start. At the first start Villeneuve accelerated straight into the lead from Hill, but Damon got sideways at the first corner, allowing both Ferraris to surge past along the following straight. Further back, Rubens Barrichello's Jordan squeezed Olivier Panis towards the right-hand wall. The Ligier driver braked hard to avoid a collision, wrong-footing Coulthard's pursuing McLaren. David slewed across to the left and Brundle was launched into his horrifying orbit over the top of the McLaren and Johnny Herbert's Sauber.

Brundle's car went hurtling end-over-end into the gravel trap on the left side of the circuit, the Peugeot engine completely breaking away from the monocoque in the huge impact. Miraculously, Brundle was able to squeeze out from beneath the upturned wreck and hurry away from the accident scene. It was the best possible advertisement for the constructional safety of Gary Anderson's chassis design on a weekend in which its lateral cockpit safety – and that of the rival Williams FW18 – had been called into question.

Hill got away cleanly at the second start, slotting in behind Villeneuve, and the two FW18s completed the opening lap half a second apart. Irvine was third, but his Ferrari was beset by understeer following a change of nose section on the grid, so he quickly moved over and allowed Schumacher through the second time round.

For most of the afternoon it was a two-horse race. Schumacher chased the Williams duo hard from the start, but only by dint of running lighter on a two-stop fuel strategy. It was the wrong way to go, but it didn't matter as the German then checked out with brake problems. That left his team-mate to come home third to wet the new Maranello baby's head on his first run for the Prancing Horse.

Start of a new dawn? As debut pole winner Jacques Villeneuve leads the pack away to start the first parade lap prior to the 1996 Australian GP at Melbourne, Eddie Irvine (2) and Michael Schumacher (1) prepare to take Ferrari into the V10-engined era with second row grid positions in their striking new F310s (ICN UK Bureau).

Schumacher had been impressed with the new John Barnard-designed F310. 'There is still some way to go,' he said. 'But yes, it went better than I expected. I had one big moment when it missed a downchange into second gear, but otherwise it ran well until the brake pedal began to go soft on me. I was pumping away at it, but it was obvious we had a big problem.' At it turned out, the culprit was eventually identified as a leaking brake pipe.

Unfortunately the immediate aftermath of the Melbourne result proved that all was still not well with the Ferrari's new slimline transmission which continued to display a propensity for developing cracks and consequent oil leaks in the next round of testing. Barnard and his team therefore argued that it would be better to concentrate on resolving the problem as quickly as possible rather than slogging on blindly and suffering public failures in races.

As a consequence, for the second round of the title chase – the Brazilian GP at Sao Paulo's wild and woolly Interlagos circuit – all three F310s were fitted with last year's transmission, suspension and undertray as a purely interim measure. It was a decision which effectively transformed the cars into little more than cobbled together 'specials'

Eddie Irvine heads for third place at Melbourne, a good start for the extrovert Ulsterman
(ICN UK Bureau).

and it would soon become obvious that any retrospective judgement as to their genuine form should not realistically take into account either of the South American races.

Even so, events in Brazil began on a bad note. In Friday free practice Eddie Irvine neatly ripped the two right-hand wheels off his car after losing control over a bump on his first out lap of the day. It was a performance which attracted a stony stare from Barnard, fresh off an overnight flight from London, but the monocoque survived intact even though the car could not be prepared in time for any further action that day.

Ferrari also took a wrong-turn in terms of chassis set-up, trying a new spring/damper set-up which Schumacher eventually reported did not improve the F310's feel. The team switched back to the Melbourne set-up for Saturday qualifying, but by then they were short of track time and Schuey did a great job muscling his way through to fourth in the final grid order.

Both he and Irvine reported their cars were bugged by considerable rear-end instability. This was further substantiated when Eddie spun during qualifying at the wheel of the spare car he'd been forced to use when his race chassis developed a fuel leak. All in all it was a pretty fraught time for the Maranello brigade.

For Schumacher, the F310 delivered less by far than he had been expecting in the race. Running a very stiff suspension set-up to secure some semblance of predictable handling, there was no question of an early change to slicks at his first refuelling stop after the Brazilian GP was started in treacherous conditions of sheeting rain.

'We had to be flexible,' he said. 'We were also lacking on straight-line speed, so a two-stop strategy was the best option for us.' He was further handicapped by poor brakes and an erratic, inconsistent gear selection.

At the end of a tiring afternoon he finished third behind a dominant Damon Hill and Jean Alesi, the man who had replaced him in the Benetton-Renault line-up. Irvine trailed home seventh. For Schumacher to be lapped by Hill shortly before the finish served as a reminder of how quickly fortunes can change in this high-octane environment. Compared with the 1995 season the winning boot was on the other foot. For the time being at least.

A week later the teams appeared at the Autodromo Oscar Galvez in Buenos Aires for the third round of the championship. In many ways the circuit recipe was much the same as Interlagos in that the surface was generally far from smooth – two bumps in particular sent spine-jarring impacts through the bottom of the cars.

Once again, Hill squeezed his Williams on to pole position, but Schumacher had set the pace from the start, wrestling his bouncing Ferrari over the bumps in a virtuoso performance which more than justified his $25 million retainer. Despite a couple of spins during the morning free practice session he had been the hero of the hour. At Interlagos the car might not have been anywhere close to the pace but here at least the German was pressing hard.

Realising that this was the only way his F310 might compete with Hill's Williams Schumacher opted for a three-stop strategy. He kept within striking distance of Damon in the opening stages before gradually dropping away into the clutches of Jean Alesi's much-improved Benetton B196.

In among the high rollers. Schumacher runs ahead of both Benettons and keeps the pressure on Hill's leading Williams in the Argentine GP, but only because he had a lighter fuel load with a three-stop strategy in mind (ICN UK Bureau).

Shortly before making his first refuelling stop at the end of lap 21, Schumacher's car may have been hit by some debris apparently thrown up by Hill's rear wheel. Either way, the rear wing flap began gradually to loosen itself, much to the detriment of the Ferrari's handling. Schumacher was given a bonus when the safety car was deployed to slow the pack after Luca Badoer rolled his Forti following a collision with Pedro Diniz's Ligier, and he managed to pull back onto Hill's tail. However eventually he stopped for good after 46 laps when the rear wing worked sufficiently loose to give him a few nasty moments out on the circuit.

Eddie Irvine came through to fifth from tenth on the grid after a gritty run with his Ferrari, but the undoubted star of the show was Jos Verstappen's Footwork which managed to edge ahead of Irvine on the last lap only to run wide and settle for a fine sixth.

'I braked too late and he repassed me,' grinned the Flying Dutchman. 'But I am very happy. I also had a moment early in the race when I lost downforce behind another car and ran wide, but I managed to get the car back onto the circuit.'

The Ferrari team returned to Maranello with mixed feelings after the South American races. The F310 was clearly off the front-running pace in this interim specification, but by the start of the European season at Nurburgring three weeks later it was Maranello's intention to field the cars in their definitive 1996 trim, complete with their original gearboxes, undertrays, and rear suspension.

Unfortunately, during that interval an apparent misunderstanding with a handful of Italian journalists resulted in an exchange of alleged insult and retraction

Schumacher eases into the cockpit prior to the start of the European GP at the Nurburgring. The car is devoid of its Marlboro sponsorship identification in deference to German rules on televised tobacco advertising (ICN UK Bureau).

between Ferrari President Luca di Montezemolo and chief designer John Barnard. The team then found itself obliged to launch what was widely interpreted as a damage limitation exercise, denying that de Montezemolo had criticised Barnard personally after the disappointing performances of the F310 in the opening races of the season.

It had initially been reported in the run-up to the European GP at Nurburgring that Montezemolo said he was 'deeply disappointed by the [F310] chassis'. However, Ferrari press officer Giancarlo Bacchini firmly rejected this, saying that Luca had actually simply remarked 'he was expecting more from the F310 – but was quite satisfied with the position in which we are. The new car arrived late, but a good result for us would be one more race win than we achieved in 1995'.

Barnard's initial reaction was to describe Montezemolo's reported observations about the chassis as 'fundamentally disruptive'. The Englishman then added: 'I don't know precisely what his words were, but it seems a pretty unhelpful thing for Luca to say'.

Barnard also commented to the author: 'To be honest, I'm a bit fed up with this pantomime, and I'm looking forward to some serious Shakespearean theatre at some time in the future. It's the usual situation. We [Ferrari Design & Development] are here as a scapegoat, and the moment something goes wrong they start popping off at us. I can only assume that there is tremendous pressure from Turin.'

These observations were reported in my sports column in *Autocar* and, on my arrival at Nurburgring, I was informed by Bacchini that Barnard was extremely annoyed by the fact that I had attributed these remarks to him. I immediately telephoned Barnard at Ferrari Design & Development and made my peace, but it was clear that his comments were founded on the basis – now apparently erroneous – that Luca had originally made the outspoken criticism. Calm was restored to the relationship. For the moment, at least.

Montezemolo carefully reserved praise for the engine department, even though there was evidence that the new 3-litre V10 was still around 30bhp down on last year's V12. 'It depends how you measure it,' says Barnard. 'Whether you take the readings from the dynamometer or calculate what it's producing when it is installed in the car.'

Barnard was also quick to remind his critics that the car which Schumacher and Irvine raced in South America was very much a special, and agreed that it was misleading to judge the overall form simply on the strength of these two races. The Englishman added that he had no knowledge of current rumours that Jordan technical director Gary Anderson had been offered a position on the Ferrari design team but had declined.

As the cars rolled out to do battle at Nurburgring, Barnard settled down to continue his wind tunnel work on the F310's cockpit and airbox, while in Maranello colleagues Gustav Brunner and Wilhelm Toet were left studying a possible new nose, side pod and diffuser configuration.

In the wake of this unhappy misunderstanding, Montezemolo paid a rare visit to a grand prix when he arrived at Nurburgring to offer his personal support to Michael Schumacher on his home soil. Luca was in an exuberant and optimistic mood, shrugging aside the rumours of a breach with Barnard.

'I have not many chances to come to the races, and in the old days I always had a very good relationship with the English press,' he joked. 'When I was running the Ferrari F1 team in the 1970s I had the Italian press always jealous because I found it sometimes easier to deal with the British!

'Apart from this, I was here at Nurburgring for the last time in the 1970s with Niki and Clay Regazzoni. Before that I competed in a very long race – 36 hours of Nurburgring – here in a Lancia Fulvia coupe. I don't even remember the date.

'Let me give you a quick picture of the situation which I now see the Ferrari F1 team facing. Last year we took a very important decision to make a V10 cylinder engine. This was to have a better power unit, not only from the viewpoint of performance, but also economy, heat dissipation, and ease of installation.

'I think we have made good progress with this engine at a time when the engine in F1 is definitely important, but less than before. I think that is demonstrated as Benetton and Williams, which both use the same engine, were almost two seconds apart in qualifying here at the Nurburgring.

'For 1996 we at Ferrari were also obliged to do a brand new car. My approach is that I generally prefer an evolutionary approach, but with the switch to the V10 cylinder engine its dimensions were very different from the V12 and we were obliged to make a totally new car from a clean sheet. To be honest, I expected altogether a more competitive car, I will admit. But on the other hand I know that it was necessary to pay a big price, particularly in the first half of the season, because we have everything new – even the fuel. The drivers, the chassis, the engine, and the gearbox.

'We know that our engine is making very steady progress, but the first priority was to make the engine reliable. Now, after the first three races we are involved in a deep investigation of the chassis in conjunction with John Barnard, because the interpretation of the rules for driver protection theoretically leave us with the possibility of having to think of a new chassis. But I sincerely hope not, both from financial and timing reasons. In the meantime, we will concentrate on working on the car which is obviously very late indeed.

'But now I want some results because we have done a lot of work. I hope to achieve our key objective to win two races this year and, if we can do this, I believe it would be realistic for us to aim for the World Championship in 1997. I think we are the best of the second division at the present time – which is not the maximum in the life but is better than nothing. We are moving step by step up the ladder of development.

'Talking about the drivers, I am extremely pleased with Schumacher, not only because he is very quick and strong in both qualifying and the race, but also because he has a very deep and good relationship with the team. He works very closely with us and motivates everybody enormously. I have a lot of experience in F1 and I have learned that the best combination is when the driver and the team can blend in to one single element altogether.

'Jean Todt is also working very well. He is a loyal and very straight man. I am very happy with his work. As for Eddie Irvine, first of all it is not easy to be team-mate to Schumacher. But they have a very easy personal relationship and this is something you can feel in the air in the team. Eddie was not able to do many tests up to now, but I am sure that he will develop into a good partner for Schumacher. He is a nice guy and very cooperative, so I am pleased.'

Montezemolo again made it clear that he was extremely satisfied with John Barnard's work – and that of all the other key personnel in the team. He confirmed that Barnard's present contract with Ferrari does not expire until August 1997 and that he was confident the partnership would continue to prosper, despite rumours of a rift with the perfectionist British engineer.

On a more personal level, Luca admitted that Ferrari was always under some pressure from the Italian press. 'That is part of the business for me,' he grinned. 'All of us, both inside and outside the company, have been expecting better. This does not mean we are suffering from a war or a tragedy.'

The Ferrari President also firmly rejected rumours that his company might be under pressure to withdraw from F1 if it did not win the World Championship in 1997. 'This is certainly a strange story,' he said with a smile. 'Ferrari has been in Formula 1 for more

Epic chase. Schumacher harries Jacques Villeneuve's Williams through a tight chicane at the Nurburgring. At the chequered flag his Ferrari was less than a second away from its first victory (Darren Heath).

than 40 years and I want the team to be competitive again, that is the priority for now. Do you think I would have invested huge amounts of money in building a new wind tunnel and recruiting young technicians with the intention of training them for the future, if it was our intention not to continue in F1?'

At the Nurburgring Damon Hill again qualified on pole, with Villeneuve second, and Schumacher third ahead of Jean Alesi's Benetton, the Jordan-Peugeot of Rubens Barrichello, and the much-improved McLaren-Mercedes of David Coulthard.

At the start Hill got badly bogged down, allowing Villeneuve to take an immediate lead, with Coulthard bursting through into an early second place. Michael was down in third place ahead of Barrichello and Hill at the end of the opening lap. Early on Jacques had things pretty much his own way, but Schumacher was right on his tail for the final 35 laps, straining every sinew to find a way past. Never more than a second behind, he hoped he might force the young French-Canadian into an error when they began lapping the backmarkers, but his big break never came.

Having blown one of the Ferrari V10s in qualifying, Schumacher had nonetheless notched up an impressive third place on the grid despite struggling with lack of mechanical grip and, in the race itself, had again proved he was in a class of his own in terms of driving genius.

The manner in which he closed up on Villeneuve after the Williams driver made his first refuelling stop was one of the most outstanding elements of the whole event. On resuming the race after refuelling on lap 26, Villeneuve found that his second set of tyres was not quite as good as the first. Meanwhile, Michael, who had made his first stop on lap 23, was indulging in the sort of quick sprint on fresh rubber which he developed as his own personal hallmark during his time with Benetton.

On his first flying lap after the stop, Villeneuve managed a 1m 23.406s. Schumacher did a 1m 21.987s. On lap 29 it was Jacques on 1m 23.130s, Michael on 1m 21.822s, and on lap 30 it was 1m 24.235s and 1m 22.019s respectively. Admittedly, Jacques was in traffic among the backmarkers at this point in the race, but it was the key moment when the battle between them almost reached a turning point.

However, it says much for Villeneuve's resilience under pressure that he simply wasn't about to be intimidated by Schumacher's presence in his mirrors. Despite pulling every trick in the book, and pressuring him relentlessly, Michael was nearly one second adrift at the chequered flag.

Montezemolo may have ventured the suggestion that, had it not been for Coulthard staying ahead of him before making his own second refuelling stop at the end of 46, Schumacher might well have won. Interestingly the German made no reference to this apparent incident and reckoned that Coulthard had driven extremely well. More crucially, Ferrari had confirmed in everyone's minds that it was fighting back. Seriously.

In that respect, the following weekend's San Marino GP at Imola may come to be seen as something of a turning point in the season – and not simply as the race in which Ferrari proved it was capable of setting the pace. It may also come to be regarded as the race at which Renault's relative lack of development progress with the RS8 V10 engine began to become apparent, and at which McLaren finally got their handling balance under control.

If anything, McLaren's improvement was even more impressive than Ferrari's. It is amazing how a good handling car can uplift a driver's spirits. At the first three races of the year David Coulthard had felt dejected. It even seemed that he was beginning to doubt his own ability. But after qualifying fourth at Imola there was a spring in his step and his face radiated a sunny mood of optimism.

Friday finished with the army of passionately enthusiastic Ferrari fans hoping that Schumacher's fastest lap in free practice was not simply a flash in the pan but a promise of what could be expected when the serious business of qualifying got under way the following day. They were not disappointed.

Schumacher's blistering pace ensured an even bigger gate than usual at the evocatively titled Autodromo Enzo e Dino Ferrari. Even so, the World Champion's determination to finish the day quickest on Friday ended when he overcooked things and spun harmlessly into a gravel trap at high speed in the closing moments of the session, matching the earlier performance of his team-mate who spun and stalled his Ferrari after clipping the kerb at one of the tricky chicanes.

On Saturday Schumacher did a brilliant job grabbing pole position from Hill in the closing moments of the hour-long qualifying session. Damon had done his best with a 1m 27.105s, but Michael managed to pull an amazing 1m 26.890s best out of the bag with only two minutes left. He even reckoned there was more to come, but seconds later spun wildly at the Tamburello chicane and came to rest with the left rear wheel leaning in at a drunken angle. Close examination revealed that the pick-up point for the rearward arm of the top left wishbone had pulled out from its mounting point on the carbon-fibre composite wing support structure bolted onto the rear of the titanium gearbox casing. The mechanics braced themselves for a long night, toiling through to 5am on Sunday to strengthen the rear end for the race.

Ironically it was the intervention of Coulthard's much improved McLaren-Mercedes which in some small measure contributed to Schumacher's frustration in the early stages of the race. Michael had clearly expected to accelerate cleanly into the lead going into the first corner but he made an uncharacteristically slow start and was passed by both the Scot and Hill going down to the first chicane.

At the end of the opening lap, Schuey sliced past Hill to take second place, but at this point Damon knew precisely what he was doing. He knew that Coulthard would hold up the Ferrari slightly and that Williams were set to beat the field on their race strategy alone.

Had Schumacher been at the head of the field he might well have enjoyed a clear enough run to get through his first refuelling stop at the end of lap 21. As it was, when he and David came in, Damon surged past and did not stop until he had completed lap 30. This convinced some observers that the Williams might only be stopping once, but Hill's car took on little more than 70 litres at the first refuelling stop.

Yet Williams had done some clever fuel consumption calculations. They had reasoned that Damon would not begin catching the backmarkers until around lap 24, after which he would be in traffic for much of the race. Thus it made sense to run the second half of the race with two shorter stints – one of 20 laps, the other of 11 – and keep the car as nimble as possible when he was in among the slower cars.

As things transpired, this was not a problem. In the second half of the race he was comfortably ahead of the opposition, the key moment in consolidating his position coming when he got out from his first stop 0.9 seconds ahead of Schumacher. Damon had no need to hurry at this point, knowing full well that all he had to do was keep calm and not allow himself to be ruffled.

That said, there were moments when Hill had things lucky. By lap 46 Schumacher found himself boxed in behind an undisciplined battle for tenth place between Mika Hakkinen's McLaren and Pedro Diniz in the Ligier. Over the course of four laps Michael lost 13 seconds before the warring duo were quite rightly called into the pits for 10-second stop-go penalties as their reward for ignoring the waved blue warning flags.

Hill took the chequered flag 16.4 seconds ahead of Schumacher, with Gerhard Berger third and Eddie Irvine

fourth. It wasn't quite the tour de force anticipated by the 130,000-strong crowd, but two Ferraris in the points was a good result by any standards – even though one of Schumacher's hard-pressed brake discs exploded mid-way round the final lap and he just managed to limp past the chequered flag before pulling off.

Schumacher had used a high-revving qualifying engine to gain pole in Ferrari's backyard, and it was announced that this would be used in the next race at Monaco. As the crowds filtered out of the Autodromo Enzo e Dino Ferrari, jamming the roads around Imola for several hours after the end of the race, they did so in a mood of high optimism.

Ferrari's F1 effort was back on the road again. With 11 rounds of the championship still to run, even though Hill – with 43 points – was now nursing a 27-point lead over Schumacher, there were even people beginning to talk in terms of Maranello's first drivers' title in 17 years. Certainly, for all the downbeat predictions at the start of the year, nobody was counting the Prancing Horse out of the running.

Schumacher speeds to second place at the San Marino GP in front of a delighted 130,000-strong crowd (Darren Heath).

Racers for the road

Even when Enzo Ferrari built the first road car carrying his own name, the Ferrari 166, in 1947, the company founder's passion was always for his racing cars. It is probably going too far to suggest that he regarded the manufacture of the road machines as something of a chore, yet it is indisputable that they funded the company's international motor racing activities throughout the 1950s and 1960s. In addition, Ferrari derived a considerable income from the manufacture and sale of sports racing cars to customers all over the world.

Today there is a relatively restricted market for competition versions of the delectable Ferrari F40, a high-performance road coupé introduced in 1987, which has been used largely in the FIA's recently instigated Global GT series. But three decades ago international World Championship endurance events had a status every bit the equal of Formula 1. And Enzo Ferrari cashed in unashamedly on both the competitiveness and charisma associated with his racing products.

Even so, by 1969 Ferrari was financially on its knees. It took Fiat President Gianni Agnelli to engineer a sympathetic marriage whereby the huge Italian volume car maker took a half share in Ferrari's company, and assumed complete responsibility for the road car manufacturing operation. The golden era of Ferrari high-performance road cars was only just beginning at this point in Maranello's history.

In the early days the great and the good who wished to buy a road-going Ferrari would often find themselves faced with no alternative but to journey to Maranello where they waited at the Commendatore's whim. If he didn't like the cut of a potential purchaser's jib, he might decide that the person concerned was simply not a suitable Ferrari owner.

It was a curious marketing strategy which, although calculated to feed the aura of mystery surrounding the cars, could hardly be regarded as commercially astute. However, by the final decade of the century such idiosyncracies have been firmly laid aside. Today a string of strategically placed dealerships throughout the world handles the sale of the Italian supercars, blending respectful gravitas with an astute sense of business.

Moreover, Ferrari is expanding. On 1 November 1995 Ferrari President Luca di Montezemolo inaugurated a sales outlet in Dubai, and the same year also saw the opening of a second outlet in China. During the first nine months of 1995 the company increased its road car sales by 25 per cent, leading to an overall production figure of 3,300 units for that year.

The Maranello factory is far from the robot-orientated environment that one might encounter at a volume road car producer. Engines are completely manufactured in-house, together with the chassis and running gear. This is mated to the shapely bodies

Work at Ferrari's road car factory on the interior finish for the exquisite F1-derived Ferrari F50 (Darren Heath).

Assembling one of the F50's V12 engines complete with transmission package. Based on the 1990 65-degree V12 Grand Prix engine, its 4.7-litre power unit develops 513bhp at 8500rpm (Darren Heath).

which are transported from the Scaglietti coachbuilders in nearby Modena, a wholly-owned subsidiary of the Ferrari organisation.

Early Ferrari production cars were virtually road-adapted racing designs fitted with coupé bodywork. They had heavy clutches, little in the way of concessions to operational comfort, and were hardly 'driveable' in the 1990s sense of the word.

The idea of a direct link between Ferrari road cars and racers may have been slightly tenuous over the past quarter century, but there have been common technical strands which related the two avenues of development. Back in the early 1970s, the delicious little Dino 246 was powered by a V6 engine which had its origins in F1 racing power units 10 years earlier, and the awesome Berlinetta Boxer of the mid-1970s would benefit from flat-12 engine technology which was closely related to the highly competitive Grand Prix engines of the time.

Yet it was not until 1995 that Ferrari announced plans for what might be described as the closest thing to a racing car for the road that the company had ever attempted. Selling in Britain for £390,000, the 513bhp, V12-engined F50 supercar can be regarded in very much the same idiom as the McLaren F1 GT ultra-performance coupé.

The F50 is more an expression of artistic and engineering excellence on a gigantic scale rather than a car in the normal sense of the word.

Crafted entirely from carbon fibre composite, the chassis employs F1 thinking to provide enormous torsional rigidity combined with light weight. Its double wishbone suspension, complete with pushrods, comes directly from the 1990/91 generation of John Barnard-inspired F1 creations and is powered by a 4.7-litre version of the 3-litre V12 engine which Alain Prost used to get within a few points of the 1990 World Championship, winning five Grands Prix in the process.

Andrew Frankel, Road Test Editor of *Autocar* magazine summed up its appeal in the following words:

'Taking to the public roads in a Ferrari F50 is a weighty responsibility...First there are the crowds; to turn up at the leaning tower of Pisa in an F50 is to glimpse what the Beatles lived with every day. I had the feeling that unless you are very careful and come with the support of both the factory and the police, you could just find yourself witnessing an F50 being loved into some very small and expensive carbon fibre fragments.

'It is the sound of that engine, not its forward thrust, which lays siege to your soul. And yet, uniquely for a Ferrari, its engine is not its greatest achievement. That honour lies with its chassis, not for the amount of grip it will generate – which is exceptional only outside the realm of the McLaren – but for its unfailingly forgiving nature.

'Luca de Montezemolo has said that the Ferrari F50 may be the last of its type. But even if this F50 is the last 200mph road car ever to poke its nose out of the Maranello factory gates, turn left and rocket up the road towards the rapidly setting sun, it can do so content in the knowledge that, as the last chapter of the story of the most remarkable road cars the world has ever produced, it has more than done justice to its genre.

'Rather more importantly, it has done its comparable marque proud too.'

The finishing touches (Darren Heath).

Index